Venicewalks

This is the
Henry Holt Walks Series,
which originated with
PARISWALKS *by Alison and Sonia Landes.*
Other titles in the series include:

LONDONWALKS *by Anton Powell*
JERUSALEMWALKS *by Nitza Rosovsky*
FLORENCEWALKS *by Anne Holler*
ROMEWALKS *by Anya M. Shetterly*
VIENNAWALKS *by J. Sydney Jones*
RUSSIAWALKS *by David and Valeria Matlock*

VENICEWALKS

Chas Carner

and

Alessandro Giannatasio

An Owl Book

Henry Holt and Company • New York

Published by Henry Holt and Company, Inc.,
115 West 18th Street, New York, New York 10011.
Published in Canada by Fitzhenry & Whiteside Limited,
195 Allstate Parkway, Markham, Ontario L3R 4T8.

Library of Congress Cataloging-in-Publication Data
Carner, Chas
Venicewalks / Chas Carner and Alessandro Giannatasio.—1st ed.
p. cm.
"An Owl book."
Includes bibliographical references.
ISBN 0-8050-1139-0
1. Venice (Italy)—Description—Tours. 2. Walking—Italy—
Venice—Guide-books. I. Giannatasio, Alessandro. II. Title.
DG672.C37 1991
914.5'3104928—dc20   90-39349
                                                      CIP

Henry Holt books are available at special discounts
for bulk purchases for sales promotions, premiums,
fund-raising, or educational use. Special editions
or book excerpts can also be created to specification.
For details contact:
Special Sales Director, Henry Holt and Company, Inc.
115 West 18th Street, New York, New York 10011

First Edition

Book design by Claire Naylon Vaccaro
Maps by Claudia Carlson

Printed in the United States of America
Recognizing the importance of preserving
the written word, Henry Holt and Company, Inc.,
by policy, prints all of its first editions
on acid-free paper. ∞
1   3   5   7   9   10   8   6   4   2

Facing title page: *View of the Grand Canal from the Accademia Bridge*

Contents

Acknowledgments

This book would never have been written—by these authors, anyway—had it not been for Cynthia Round, known as Cinzia to her many loving friends in Italy. It was she who first conceived of the idea, who first provided the research materials, introductions, connections, guidance, criticism, suggestions, and encouragement to make this project a reality. Her knowledge of, and love for, Italian history, life-style, art, culture, food, wine, people, religion, and language—and her generous sharing of that knowledge—provided the inspiration for this work. It is with warm hearts that we say, *Mille grazie, cara Cinzia. Ti siamo grati.*

Thanks and appreciation to Kevin McShane, our agent at Fifi Oscard Associates, for handling the business side of things; to Theresa Burns, our editor at Henry Holt, for her involvement and support on this project; and to associates Ricki Stern, William Rexer, and Jeffrey Good, whose research work proved efficient and insightful.

Thanks also to Lino Nisianakis, Luciano Santini, and Bruno Fagarazzi; special people who graciously opened their hearts and homes and who make Venice an even more wonderful place in which to live. And to Carla and Roberto Cagliero, more thanks still, for their lifelong friendship and generous contributions to this work.

Finally, a loving thank you to Ann L. Carner, who instilled within one writer a sense of wonder and wanderlust that shall always enrich his days.

May this book widen the horizons of everyone!

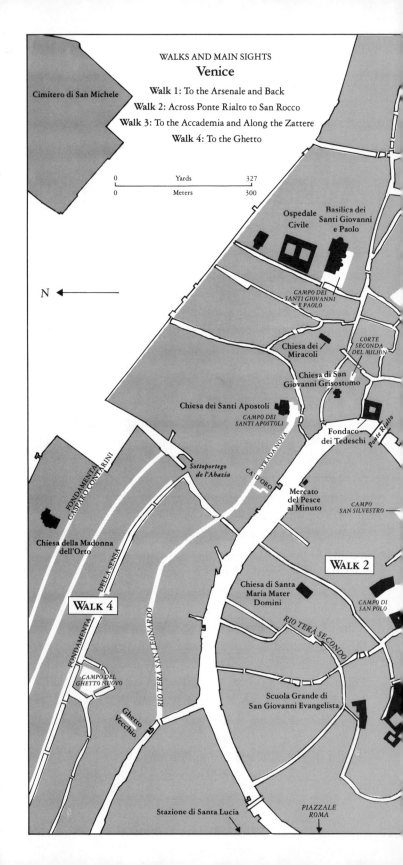

WALKS AND MAIN SIGHTS
Venice

Walk 1: To the Arsenale and Back
Walk 2: Across Ponte Rialto to San Rocco
Walk 3: To the Accademia and Along the Zattere
Walk 4: To the Ghetto

Cimitero di San Michele

| 0 | Yards | 327 |
| 0 | Meters | 300 |

N ◄─────

Ospedale Civile
Basilica dei Santi Giovanni e Paolo

CAMPO DEI SANTI GIOVANNI E PAOLO

Chiesa dei Miracoli

CORTE SECONDA DEL MILION

Chiesa di San Giovanni Grisostomo

Chiesa dei Santi Apostoli

CAMPO DEI SANTI APOSTOLI

Fondaco dei Tedeschi

Ponte Rialto

Sottoportego de l'Abazia

CA' D'ORO

STRADA NOVA

Mercato del Pesce al Minuto

CAMPO SAN SILVESTRO

FONDAMENTA GASPARO CONTARINI

Chiesa della Madonna dell'Orto

DELLA SENSA

WALK 4

FONDAMENTA

WALK 2

Chiesa di Santa Maria Mater Domini

CAMPO DI SAN POLO

RIO TERA SECONDO

RIO TERA SAN LEONARDO

CAMPO DEL GHETTO NUOVO

Ghetto Vecchio

Scuola Grande di San Giovanni Evangelista

Stazione di Santa Lucia

PIAZZALE ROMA

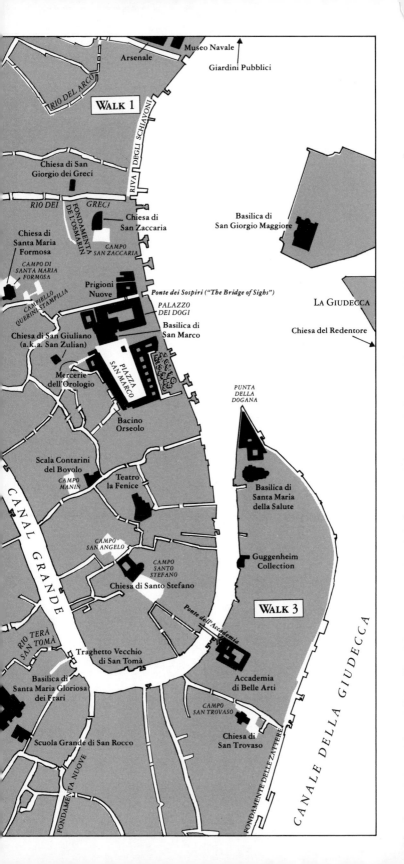

Arsenale

Museo Navale

Giardini Pubblici

WALK 1

Chiesa di San Giorgio dei Greci

RIO DEL ARCO

RIO DEI GRECI

FONDAMENTA DE L'OSMARIN

Chiesa di Santa Maria Formosa

CAMPO DI SANTA MARIA FORMOSA

CAMPIELLO QUERINI STAMPALIA

Chiesa di San Zaccaria

CAMPO SAN ZACCARIA

RIVA DEGLI SCHIAVONI

Basilica di San Giorgio Maggiore

LA GIUDECCA

Prigioni Nuove

Ponte dei Sospiri ("The Bridge of Sighs")

PALAZZO DEI DOGI

Chiesa del Redentore

Chiesa di San Giuliano (a.k.a. San Zulian)

Basilica di San Marco

Mercerie dell'Orologio

PIAZZA SAN MARCO

Bacino Orseolo

PUNTA DELLA DOGANA

Scala Contarini del Bovolo

CAMPO MANIN

Teatro la Fenice

Basilica di Santa Maria della Salute

CANAL GRANDE

CAMPO SAN ANGELO

CAMPO SANTO STEFANO

Guggenheim Collection

Chiesa di Santo Stefano

WALK 3

RIO TERÀ SAN TOMÀ

Ponte dell'Accademia

Traghetto Vecchio di San Tomà

Basilica di Santa Maria Gloriosa dei Frari

Accademia di Belle Arti

CAMPO SAN TROVASO

CANALE DELLA GIUDECCA

Scuola Grande di San Rocco

Chiesa di San Trovaso

FONDAMENTA NUOVE

FONDAMENTE DELLE ZATTERE

Venicewalks

Introduction

This book is designed to show you a Venice very few visitors ever see. It's an invitation for you to step away from the major sites crammed with foreigners, and to enter more intimately the *sestieri*, districts, that are the real Venice. You are about to experience a life-style and an atmosphere unique in the world, one both ancient and modern, hectic and serene, cosmopolitan and insular, frivolous and wise.

Each of these four walks is plotted to steer you away from crowded and obvious tourist attractions and guide you through areas where the Venetian people live. Hidden within each of these neighborhoods are works of art and architecture as precious as any in Venice's museums and major churches. And these treasures are held most dearly by the Venetians themselves, because the works are a part of their everyday lives; they keep alive—and living—a heritage too easily considered static and frozen in a time long ago.

According to the Venetian tourist board, during the seven-month peak season from April through October, an average of 90,000 sightseers comes to the city every day. They arrive by hydroplane, cruise liner, private yacht, ferryboat, plane, train, bus, car, and bicycle. Representing all nationalities, races, religions, and political persuasions and speaking all languages, they pack the area around Piazza San Marco. And for a city of fewer than 90,000 natives, this constitutes a significant daily invasion. Most here accept this confluence of humanity as hopefully as they do the movements of the tides.

Yet as proof of Venice's exclusivity—intimacy, if you will—here's an interesting statistic: with fewer than 10,000 hotel beds available, eight out of nine tourists in Venice spend an average of only six hours there.

If you plan to be one of these people, read this book carefully in advance and, according to your strongest interests, select only one or two of these approximately three-hour walks. (On your next visit you'll get to the others. And meanwhile you'll have the chance to read about them.) The rest of your time is truly best spent around Piazza San Marco: snapping pictures, buying souvenirs, eating *gelato*, feeding pigeons, maybe riding in a gondola. Be sure to tour the Basilica (and do *not* neglect to venture upstairs to see the original Four Horses), visit the Doges' Palace, see the Bridge of Sighs, climb the Campanile, linger over lunch in a neighborhood *trattoria*, wander over to Ponte Rialto and splurge a little in the countless gift shops selling masks, jewelry, glassware, lace, antiques, artwork, trinkets, and postcards. Otherwise, with so little time and so much to do, one can easily run the risk of biting off more than can be chewed, seeing too much and appreciating too little.

If you are lucky enough to be staying in Venice twenty-four hours or longer, you'll find that combinations of these walks mix nicely together: one in the morning, one in the afternoon.

Each of the four walks covers various eras in Venetian cultural, political, and economic history. And as we weave and wander in all directions about this city, the evolution of Venetian life will unfold.

It is our contention that Venice is the most pedestrian-friendly community in the world, although you may not think so upon first impression. No matter how you reach this city (see the section on Transportation, page 11), you will enter its heart from the water. Carrying your overpacked luggage, you will float along the Grand Canal—by waterbus, watertaxi, or gondola—stare out at imposing palaces and churches, and wonder how anyone negotiates this town without a pair of waterwings. But the truth is that every site in Venice is reached easily on foot, and that is what this book is designed to help you accomplish. As James Russell Lowell wrote to his friend Thomas Hughes on Thanksgiving 1873: "The canals only give one a visiting acquaintance. The *calli* [streets] make you an intimate of the household."

If you arrive before midday, as most people do, you will reach your destination, disembark amid throngs of sight-seers, and step on *"terraferma."* (We keep that term in quotation marks because—as you'll learn over these four walks—*nothing* in Venice is on "solid ground." Everything has been constructed on hundreds of millions of ancient wooden pylons sunk into the sediment of the Lagoon.)

Where do you go? What do you do? How do you get there? ("In Venice, there is no north and south"—this is a common expression.)

You stop for a beat, sit on your suitcases, and open the map you have, wisely, brought with you. We can almost hear the gasp as you register the contorted maze of pas-sageways that would chagrin the Minotaur himself. Be calm. And keep this in mind: The whole city could fit in New York City's Central Park; nothing is very far away.

If you are in dire need, somewhere nearby you will find—or be found by—a gentleman wearing a cap and possibly equipped with a hand truck. He is a *facchino*, porter, who will transport your luggage and guide you to your hotel. Undoubtedly, out of gratitude and relief, you

3

will tip him too much (see the section on Tipping on page 21).

Once checked in and settled, you will spend your first hours in Venice doing what most tourists do here: what we have described above. With map close at hand, quickly you will begin to register and recognize landmarks that will assure an easy return to your lodgings. And just as quickly, we trust, you will grow restless and tired of the crowd's confinement. By day's end, you will want to venture out on your own. Congratulations, you've taken the first step toward meeting the real Venice. *Benvenuti a Venezia!*

And the "real Venice" begins to emerge around seven-thirty in the evening, when most *stranieri*, foreigners, have gone back to where they came from. Offices and shops close their doors for the day; coffee bars, wine bars, and restaurants open theirs for the night. During this cheerful and peaceful time of day the *passeggiata*, evening stroll, takes place: a chance to move and mingle among the natives as they reclaim the city for themselves, just as the swallows reclaim the sky overhead.

In the neighborhood *campi*, or squares, near Ponte Rialto, you'll see the teenagers first. Hundreds of them: healthy, bright, attractive, and impeccably dressed. Walking quietly arm in arm, they are the students, shop clerks, and office staffers who have ended their workday, hurried home, and changed their clothes and who now congregate in friendly groups. They do outside what most kids their age do at home: catch up on news of the day, trade tidbits of gossip, discuss sports scores, make plans for the weekend, nurse eager hearts bruised by puppy love, embrace in shadowy recesses out of view of their parents. In the fresh air and golden twilight, it all seems wholesome and easy.

You'll find the grown-ups nearby, standing just inside the door of their favorite *enoteca*, wine bar, and doing much the same as their adolescent children. Step inside and join them; order a glass of *Prosecco*, a lightly sparkling, dry white wine; nibble a few of the ever-present (and always stale) potato chips at the bar.

Here—as elsewhere in Venice—you will find someone to join you in pleasant conversation, whether you speak Italian or not. In fact, it is not uncommon to meet natives who speak three, four, five different languages. Such is the heritage of a city that has been the world's crossroads for twelve centuries.

Give yourself a little time here and relax, feel at home, before strolling off to another wine bar that suits your liking. It's still too early to worry about dinner, but as you move along the *calli*, sidestepping young children playing under their grandparents' proud and watchful eyes, take note of restaurants to which you may want to return. Watch the waiters swoop through and set up their tables with meticulous professionalism. Scan the menus. Choose your table. By eight or eight-thirty they'll be ready to seat you.

Along each of these walks, we will be pointing out restaurants you may want to patronize for lunch or dinner or both. For the most part, they're modestly priced and traditional. And while you won't find their names in most visitor's guides, they're known by Venetians to be among the best for what they serve.

Among natives, the feast of the day is the midday meal. Schools close around noon or 12:30, and businesses take a pause from 12:30 to 15:30 or 16:00 (3:30 or 4:00); and families commune around the dining table. But most visitors here content themselves with a light lunch and a long, luxurious meal in the evening. In this way, Venetian hospitality is most appreciated.

Seafood is the specialty of the city: fresh from the Lagoon, and savory whether it is fried, grilled, or poached. It finds its way into most of five courses—*antipasto*, *primo*, *secondo*, sometimes even the *contorno* (but not the dessert, *dolce*)—and one would be unwise, indeed, to avoid it. Undoubtedly, you will discover personal favorites, which you may reorder in different restaurants throughout your stay. But each establishment has its own specialty of the house, and these should be tried as well.

In the company of friends and loved ones, three hours over dinner is not a long time in Venice. It is very much a part of the daily cycle here. And it is only by living through the full cycle of a day that one can see Venice as it really is.

When you eventually make your way back to your hotel, you will be bathed in moonlight and a glorious silence unlike any you have ever known. The streets are safe although empty. The quiet is soothing although alien. The night is benign although mysterious. Soon enough, you will be asleep in your bed, but maybe you should first revisit Piazza San Marco while it is vacant and vast. You'll be glad you did. . . .

Venice awakens at seven, when countless bells in countless churches ring in the day. By 7:05, when the last *gong* has echoed down the nearest canal and faded away, the staccato *clack-clack, clack-clack* of wooden shutters flung open against stone façades sets a high rhythm to the basso voices of so many boat engines starting the day's work.

A neighbor sings in her kitchen. A young moving-man calls up from on deck to his partner still asleep. Nearby, a boat horn sounds—surprisingly like an automobile's and therefore out of place here—and alerts the visitor to an eagerness all around to begin the rituals of morning.

The *click-click* of hard heels down narrow alley streets. The piercing *tweet*s of swallows nesting under roof tiles mix with the gurgling *coo*s of the ubiquitous pigeons. A child whines. Another laughs. And the first warning call of *"Hoi-ay . . . hoi-ay"* is heard from a gondolier approaching around a blind right angle.

A soft gray light fills the room. You pull the lace-trimmed sheet close under your chin against the cool dampness of a gentle breeze through your window. All to no avail. Because by seven-thirty the bells begin again, to convince you that—no matter how late the night before—this day begins anew and it begins *now*.

Information
and Advice

ABOUT THIS BOOK

We have created a narrative guide to Venice as rich in
information as could fit into this volume. It must be carried on each of the walks. And it is best skimmed prior
to your arrival there.

Along with *Venicewalks*, you should carry a detailed
map of the city, an Italian dictionary, and possibly another type of reference book (see the Bibliography on
page 213). Two excellent maps are available free of charge
from the Azienda di Promozione Turistica (APT), the
tourist information office located in the Ala Napoleonica
(Walk 2) in Piazza San Marco (tel. 5226356).

As you read through each section in preparation for
a walk, keep a pencil handy. Write in the margins; high-
light passages you'll want to read again on site; circle
references to special landmarks; underscore historical or
biographical information.

Use the book as a journal as well. Throughout your
visit, scribble thoughts and sketches, dates, names and

addresses, questions and answers, corrections and suggestions, ideas and observations, updatings and changes, wherever there's white space. Make it your own and personally improve it. May it be a well-loved souvenir when you return home.

EMERGENCIES

Heaven forbid, but it's best to put this information right up front.

Police/Fire/Ambulance: Dial **113** from any phone; you'll be asked which service you need.

Hospitals: Civili Riuniti di Venezia: Campo Santi Giovanni e Paolo, tel. 705622 or 707556

Ospedale al Mare: Lungomare D'Annunzio, Lido, tel. 761750

Lost passport: Contact the police, then your consulate:

Austria—4700 San Marco, tel. 32133 or 700459

Belgium—5768 Cannaregio, tel. 5224124

Denmark—2347 San Polo, tel. 706822

Finland—San Giuliano, tel. 59912

France—1397 Dorsoduro, tel. 5222392 or 5224319

Germany—2888 San Marco, tel. 5225100

Greece—720 San Polo, near the Rialto Bridge, tel. 5237260

Netherlands—4150 Castello, Riva degli Schiavoni, tel. 38112

Norway—127 Lungo Rotondo Garibaldi, Mestre, tel. 962050

Spain—2442 San Marco, tel. 87877 or 704510

Sweden—499 Santa Croce, Piazzale Roma, tel. 706888 or 791611

Switzerland—810 Dorsoduro, near the Accademia, tel. 5225996

United Kingdom—1051 Dorsoduro, near the Accademia, tel. 27207 or 27408

United States—Largo Donegan 1, Milan, tel. (02) 652841

Others—Contact office in Rome.

American Express: San Marco 1471, near San Moisè, tel. 700844

Also, should you need it, keep in mind that the Venice phone book is widely accessible beyond the main post office; you can consult it at practically any bar, restaurant, hotel, or retail store.

DOCUMENTATION

From the United States, for a visit of three months or less, only a valid passport is required. (Come 1992, all Europeans should be able to use an EEC passport.) Vaccination certificates are no longer necessary.

To drive in Italy, you'll need a valid U.S. driver's license and a permit from the Italian State Tourist Office (ENIT), also available through most motoring organizations (although we've never been called upon to present it in Italy).

TRANSPORTATION

Cruise liners set and hoist anchor night and day. Their specific docking locations are allotted to various companies, which operate on their own schedules. Most liners are moored within strolling distance of Piazza San Marco.

Planes from overseas fly into Milan or Rome. Certain flights from within Italy and Europe arrive at Venice's Marco Polo Airport. Alitalia has recently begun direct flights from New York to Venice.

Watertaxis are available to carry you from Marco Polo Airport to Piazza San Marco. They cost about $70 one way and take about an hour. Another motorboat service

transports passengers between San Marco and the airport. It costs 11,000 lire. Shuttle buses, which are *much* cheaper, run between the airport and Piazzale Roma as well (5,000 lire, and about two hours total).

Trains arrive at and depart from Santa Lucia Railway Station (train information office open 7:00–22:40; tel. 715555) at the Piazzale Roma end of the Grand Canal. After rolling over the Veneto mainland, you'll pass through industrialized Mestre and over a long lagoon causeway and into the station. You'll descend the wide stone steps outside and—for about $1.50—board a *vaporetto*, waterbus (no. 1, "Per San Marco," 1,800 lire), to your destination.

Public parking space is located on mainland Mestre (where you'll connect with Venice via train) and at Piazzale Roma at the western end of Venice itself. Whether you're driving or riding a bus, you will motor over the long causeway and disembark here before entering Venice along the Grand Canal. The parking lot is just one *vaporetto* stop from the train station.

A number of car-rental offices are located at Piazzale Roma, and many people drop off one-way rentals here after touring northern Italy or pick up a car after their

Venetian visit to begin the next leg of their vacation. If you are parking a car and will reclaim it after your visit, we strongly suggest that you leave it on the mainland (Mestre) and take the train into Venice. Prices at Piazzale Roma are many times over those of mainland lots. Another driving note: discount gas coupons are available through various motor clubs and the Italian State Tourist Office (ENIT) and at border crossings. Take the time to look into them; they can save you some money.

Vaporetti form the backbone of Venetian public transportation and are the cheapest means of reaching nearly all points in the city. Stops along the Grand Canal are frequent and alternate side to side. A schedule and a map are posted at every stop.

Vaporetto no. 1 is the Grand Canal local; it costs 1,800 lire and leaves each stop about every ten minutes. It makes all of the stops from Tronchetto, at the farthest (western) end of the Canal, to Piazza San Marco and Lido island. Although crowded at rush hour, it is the best way to get around. *Especially for your first ride along the Canal Grande, be sure to ride outside.*

The no. 34 is added as an auxiliary line between June 15 and October 15. It, too, leaves every ten minutes and costs 1,800 lire; it is slightly quicker, however, making fewer stops along the way.

The no. 5, the *circolare*, or circle line (Walk 1), circumnavigates the city on boats leaving every thirty minutes. It avoids the Grand Canal and is a very good way to see Venice from all sides. It, too, costs 1,800 lire.

The no. 12 (tel. 5287886) leaves on the hour from Fondamenta Nuove and carries passengers to out-islands such as Murano, Torcello, and Burano. (If you can take an afternoon, visit these islands; they are very special.) One-way costs 2,500 lire.

Apart from the standard fares, discount tickets are available. A twenty-four-hour pass costs 10,000 lire and offers unlimited access for one day. A seventy-two-hour ticket costs 17,000 lire.

Private watertaxis (tel. 32326 or 22303) can be hired throughout the city, but be advised that many visitors have complained of the high fares. A ten-minute ride can cost $40.

Gondola rates are regulated by the city; make sure both you and the gondolier agree on the price before embarking. A fifty-minute ride will cost close to $60. A ride in one of these legendary boats is an invaluable experience. Select the proper hour (sundown, evening), don't worry about the cost, and bring along a favorite bottle of wine.

WARDROBE

Nowhere else in Europe does the concept of sensible shoes apply better than in Venice. Besides an occasional *vaporetto* ride on the Grand Canal, your principal means of transportation are your feet. And unless you're in sturdy shape, your feet, legs, and lower back soon will remind you just how unused they are to the "normal" daily workout of getting around town.

Every public space—*calle*, *campo*, *fondamenta*—is paved in stone. Every *ponte*, bridge, is approached by *scalini*, stairs. Sometimes these surfaces are uneven; after a rain, many are slick and slippery. Soft soles (preferably rubber) and low heels are both the fashion and the time-tested mode of footwear. Bring two pairs: light and supportive sports shoes for day, dressy and comfortable leather shoes for night. (And ladies, trust us on this, please: Unless you intend to carry them to a formal event and change into them there, high heels do *not* work in Venice.)

Pack sparingly, for a number of reasons. Obviously, there are the benefits of greater mobility, security, and self-sufficiency. In addition, Italian baggage handlers are notorious for their frequent, scheduled *scioperi*, strikes. If you can get away with carry-on luggage, you may very well spare yourself a long and frustrating wait in the airport. Once you reach the city and discover how much walking you will have to do, you'll be glad you packed lightly as you make your way through the many alleys and stairways to your hotel room. A collapsible luggage cart (with large wheels) and a small folding umbrella are good to bring along as well.

In tourist season, Venice's climate is a lot like that of New York City during the spring and summer: warm and randomly rainy in the early months (50°–70°F/10°–21°C), hot and humid later in the season (62°–80°F/17°–27°C).

Venetians are stylish and casual in their dress; they layer their clothing with a sweater or jacket if the temperature gets cool. Shorts are a good idea in the summer, but only if you plan to spend your day outside; most churches will not allow adults wearing shorts inside their doors. Nor will they tolerate tank tops on women; it is advisable to exercise a little modesty in dress.

Venetian winters (32°–53°F/0°–12°C) are comparatively mild, rainy and almost cold; snow is a rarity. From December through February, a wool jacket or overcoat is recommended. For the rest of the year, an all-purpose jacket or raincoat should suffice.

Among Venetians, suits for men and formal business attire for women are reserved strictly for office hours and worn almost exclusively by professionals. At night, a sport jacket—with or without a tie—or a comfortable dress will get you into almost any establishment.

DIRECTIONS

In Venice, you will get lost. Expect it. Enjoy it. Rely more on your senses of curiosity, humor, abandon, and less on those of direction and control. And carry a good map. ("To be lost is to find," as has been said many times here.)

Even if you are entangled amid linguine-thin alleyways, how lost can you be in a city such as this? One

All roads lead to St. Mark's

can walk from any end of Venice to another in less than an hour. Even a "wrong" street will lead you quickly to a bearings-setting landmark. And after your simple *"Mi scusi, dov'è . . . ?"*—"Excuse me, where is . . . ?"—a native will be pleased to show you the way.

"Sempre diritto"—"Merely straight ahead"—is the legendary and traditional response to any visitor's inquiry concerning directions around Venice. And as we will learn shortly, it has also been a Venetian in-joke for about twelve hundred years.

Nowadays, *"sempre diritto"* usually precedes a long series of hand signals indicating right, *a destra*, and left, *a sinistra*. Often, when the direction-seeker's face tenses with confusion and anxiety, the direction-giver will generously lead the way.

If all else fails, remember this: All roads lead to Ponte Rialto and Piazza San Marco, the foci of Venice. Signs pointing toward either are overhead everywhere in the city. If you anticipate becoming separated from your party, merely agree ahead of time at which site and what time you will meet; you will be reunited easily and quickly.

16

While making your way through the twists and turns of the city, you will notice that everything in Venice—even the smallest bridge, shortest alleyway, or lowest *sottoportego*, underpass—has a name. (Just for the record, there are some 400 bridges, 3,000 streets, 150 canals, and 117 islands in Venice.) Do not despair, or try to remember them all. The natives have had twelve centuries to label each and every one (sometimes with a handle longer than the passageway itself).

Many maps and guidebooks do a relatively good job of recording the compulsive nomenclature, but the spelling of these names often varies; certain of these we have standardized. The names of locations mentioned in this book have, whenever possible, been taken from the signs themselves.

One final logistical note: The starting point for all four of the walks is **Piazza San Marco**. Since every other public square in Venice is referred to as a *campo* (literally, "field") it is the only Piazza in Venice and is easily the most recognizable landmark for all visitors. Also, since many hotels are located near Piazza San Marco, it is a most accessible point of departure and return.

HEALTH

Although most homes, bars, and restaurants prefer to serve *acqua minerale* (still or sparkling) mineral water, you *can* drink the water in Venice. What poured through the faucets in olden times was rainwater, collected in cisterns and filtered through sand and clay; now it comes from the hills of the Veneto through huge viaducts.

The canals do, indeed, carry the city's refuse out to sea, so don't plan on going for any midnight swims. The canals are flushed out twice a day by the tides; they suffer more from detergent pollution (from the many restaurants, among others) than from anything else.

The food in Venice is healthful and served proudly.

The air is clean and wafted by breezes off the Adriatic.

If you should find yourself in need of a physician or pharmacy, check with your hotel's front desk for a recommendation. Doctors speaking languages other than Italian are usually on call. The Ospedale Civile (see "Emergencies," page 10), provides first aid twenty-four hours a day, but if a major medical emergency exists, make plans to move to a mainland hospital (in Milan, Florence, or Rome, for example) as quickly as possible.

MONEY

The currency in Italy is the lira, whose value fluctuates—daily—against that of other countries. At the time of this writing, the exchange rate stood at about 1,100 lire to the dollar; six years earlier, it stood at close to 1,800. The lira is relatively strong across world markets. Visitors should not expect to find bargains here. (Indeed, many Italians now make their major purchases of clothing and photographic and electronic goods on trips to the United States, since they can save anywhere from one-quarter to one-third with the exchange rate.)

We recommend that you carry an adequate supply of widely accepted traveler's checks (American Express, Thomas Cook, Barclays, and Citibank are the most widely accepted) and at least one major credit or charge card (Visa, MasterCard, American Express, or Diners Club) on your trip.

Change currency in small amounts on various days throughout your stay to take advantage of better rates. *Remember that most currency exchange offices are closed on Sunday; those at airports and train stations usually remain open.*

Venetian banks are generally open weekdays, 8:30–13:30 and 15:00–16:00, but not all offer money-changing services. Many a tourist has spent a lot of time in a long line only to discover that he's wasted it in a place that cannot help him. So be advised and ask first at the information desk before stepping into a line.

You can usually change money at your hotel's front desk, but it will not give as good a return as an *ufficio di cambio*, or foreign-exchange office. There are a number of these establishments in or near Piazza San Marco. Because they operate exclusively for this purpose and compete for tourists' business, they offer the best deals and the easiest, quickest service. Such shops are scattered all over the city and can easily be spotted by the "Cambio" sign displayed out front.

As you plan your budget (for two), figure $100–$300 per day for a hotel and $100–$200 per day for food and wine.

You'll collect a fair amount of spare change during your time in Venice. It's good to keep it handy. Practically every major museum and some churches charge an admission fee. Once you are inside, audio guides and coin-operated illumination systems (generally costing 200–500 lire) provide appreciated enhancement to certain exhibited works of art.

STAMPS, TICKETS, TOKENS, AND TOBACCO

The main post office is located in the Fondaco dei Tedeschi at the eastern end of Ponte Rialto (Walk 2); there are about a dozen other offices scattered around the city's six districts. Mailboxes are found on the streets and in major squares.

For quick service in purchasing stamps and pay-phone tokens—*francobolli* and *gettoni*, respectively (good things to carry in your pocket or purse)—frequent the little stores that display a black rectangular sign with a large T in white. These are tobacconist's shops, which are authorized by the government to sell such regulated commodities as tobacco, postage stamps, tokens, public-transportation passes, and—believe it or not—salt, governmental control of which hails back to well before the Middle Ages.

We recommend these shops especially for stamps, because the lines in post offices are notoriously long and confusing. If you do use the post office, be sure to ask which line is which before committing to any one. (An airmail postcard stamp to the United States currently goes for 850 lire. Count on a card's taking two to three weeks to reach its U.S. destination.)

If you're a smoker, you will learn quickly to plan ahead and buy your tobacco goods at these shops during normal business hours. Once their doors close, for the night, usually at seven-thirty, you're out of luck. There are no vending machines in the city, and although we know of two bars in Venice that do sell cigarettes "under the counter" after hours as a courtesy to customers and friends, we are obliged not to divulge their names or locations.

FOOD AND WINE

"There is no bad food in Venice," a friend of ours is fond of saying, and she's right. But one rule almost always applies: The farther away from Piazza San Marco, the better the food and the lower the price. For this reason alone, you should invest time exploring areas beyond your immediate neighborhood, no matter where you happen to be staying.

A cup of coffee will cost you between 1,000 and 2,500 lire. A bottle of water, about 1,500. A good pizza, 12,000–20,000. A cola, 2,000. A sandwich, 1,500–3,000. Ice cream, 1,500–2,000.

Many restaurants offer a fixed-price tourist's menu, which generally is reasonably priced but uninspired fare. To all but the least adventuresome diner, we recommend that you order à la carte and favor the seafood dishes for which Venice is so renowned.

In the types of restaurants we'll introduce, lunch for two, with wine, will go for 42,000–60,000 lire; dinner, 50,000 or more.

(See the list of Italian and Venetian food and wine terms, beginning on page 29.)

TIPPING

A service charge of one form or another is already added to just about every restaurant bill (indicated as *"coperto e servizio"*) and hotel bill ("IVA"), so tipping at these establishments is modest: less than 10 percent for a meal, and 2,000 lire per day for maids.

A reasonable fee for a porter is 15,000–25,000 lire. The amount depends, of course, on the degree of difficulty in getting your luggage from point A to point B.

A note about restaurants: Some years ago, the Italian government confronted head-on the problem of tax collection within this heavily cash-oriented industry (restaurateurs everywhere are notoriously lax in their bookkeeping) and came up with an ingenious solution. The responsibility of obtaining—and retaining—meal receipts was placed on the *customers*, who are required by law to carry these chits to within a hundred meters of the front door of an establishment. Departing diners may be stopped by a police officer and asked to show a record of payment for their meal. So remember to carry that slip of paper with you as you step outside.

SHOPPING

You'll find it all, here in Venice. From the finest designer shops to the smartest original boutiques. From the latest innovations to pieces from classic historical eras. A general rule: Prices compare favorably to those of other major cities for textile and leather goods, but are higher than in other cities for jewelry, sunglasses, electronic gadgets, and photographic equipment. Uniquely Venetian lace, glassware, paper products, and antiques are priced at a premium, but that should surprise no one.

Shops are generally open from 9:00 to 13:00 and 15:30 to 19:30; days closing vary. From May through October, "downtown" shops around San Marco are open from 10:00 to 19:30 seven days a week.

In addition to cash and cards, some shops and restaurants accept traveler's checks as payment. If you have large items shipped directly home, you may avoid the IVA, or value-added tax.

TIME

Venice is an hour ahead of Greenwich Mean Time, and thus six hours ahead of Eastern (U.S.) Time.

As you've probably already noticed, time references in this book are based on the twenty-four-hour clock. (One o'clock in the afternoon is rendered "13:00," and so on.)

In spite of what one might think about Italians "in general," Venetians are *extremely* punctual people. If the timetable at a *vaporetto* stop says the boat departs at 6:05, it will. If the ticketman at the train station says the train pulls out at 15:36, it's gone by 15:37. If the gondoliers go on strike from 10:00 to 12:00, the first boat pulls out of its slip at 12:00:01.

This is a city with no traffic jams or stalled elevators to screw up a schedule. For twelve hundred years, the natives have been walking these streets; they know exactly how long it takes to get anywhere in the city. If you agree to meet someone at a particular time in some obscure *campo*, you will likely find him waiting patiently for you and have to start your greeting with an apology for being late. He will politely, understandingly shake your hand without even a glance at his watch.

Zodiacal clock of the Torre dell'Orologio

For the tourist, Venetian punctuality applies most noticeably to opening hours of shops, museums, banks, government and business offices, you name it. A general rule of thumb: Between 12:30 and 15:30, all systems are down. Never mind that midday is prime time for sightseers; it's lunchtime for all of Venice, all of Italy. And for this reason, we have designed these walks to be taken before or after the customary break in the day. This is an important consideration when scheduling your walks.

PHOTOGRAPHY

Venice is a City of Light. The sun's rays glance off waves and shimmer on ceilings, glow golden off church façades and shine warmly down long, narrow streets. Any photograph you take here will be a treasure.

But be advised: The use of flashes and tripods is not allowed in most churches and museums, so you will have to master your hand-holding or timer techniques. Some black-and-white films are rated up to 3200 ASA nowadays, and color print films are getting faster all the time, so you can do some pretty amazing stuff.

A small zoom lens—28-to-85mm, for example—provides excellent flexibility and allows you to capture the vastness of Piazza San Marco or the detail of a fragment of church sculpture.

Slide-shooters, remember that Kodachrome—25, 64, 200 ASA—is neither sold nor processed overseas. Ektachrome and films of other major manufacturers are available just about anywhere in Europe and are found easily in the shops of Venice. Even street vendors sell 135 and 110 film (but check the expiration dates on the boxes before buying).

Try "pushing" positive (slide) film by adjusting your camera's ASA dial setting: 25 ASA to 30, 64 to 80, 200 to 250, for example. This "fools" the camera into shooting just a tad faster, prevents an excess of white light from washing out the image, and thus saturates it with vivid color. Process film shot this way as standard issue. Images will be of superior quality, color, and clarity.

MISCELLANEOUS

Look up, but look out. Venetians are some of the cleanest people in the world. Unfortunately, their culture has not yet embraced the practice of cleaning up after pets. It's a pity, really, because the streets and courtyards are otherwise litter-free. As you make your way around the city, take note of the beautiful flowers cascading from window boxes, colorful laundry fluttering in the breeze, intricate façades, unique fluted chimneys, and characteristic rooftop terraces, *altane*, overhead. But do not do so without first scoping out a clear path underfoot!

Communication among Venetians is refreshingly direct, and it rubs off on their dealings with their countless visitors. This directness is one of the many bonuses to enjoy in a cosmopolitan yet homogeneous culture such as Venice. Eye contact is trusting and friendly. A smile is offered simply and returned easily. Conversations begin naturally from there.

If you're a whistler, you'll love strolling the narrow *calli* of Venice. But you'll be in stiff competition; good whistlers are bred right here at home. For sixty generations, Venetians have been learning the acoustics of the city, how the sound waves reflect off walls and canals. And even some among the youngest know a full repertoire of operas. (But don't let that stop you. Music is always appreciated.)

Public toilets are woefully scarce and poorly maintained in Venice, but fear not. You need not scurry around the streets looking for that elusive "WC"; the price of a cup of coffee will entitle you to use a restaurant or café's rest room. Another helpful hint: Carry little packets of facial tissues in your pocket or purse. Toilet paper in Italy can be of poor quality (rough) and is sometimes nonexistent.

COMMONLY USED ITALIAN AND VENETIAN TERMS

Every region of Italy has its own accent and language; even an untrained ear can discern the differences. And Venice proudly harbors its own. Much of the language here shows the influence from the many cultures that have mixed here throughout the centuries; there are words derived from, among others, Greek, Arabic, Spanish, Turkish, and German. To get an idea of how different Venetian can be from Italian, consider the word for "fork": in Venetian it is *piron*, while the Italian is *forchetta*.

General

acqua: water
altana: rooftop terrace
arrivederci: farewell, so long
basilica: major church of historical importance
battello: waterbus or boat
biglietto: ticket
buona notte: good night
buona sera: good evening
buon giorno: good day; good morning
bottega: store
ca': short for *casa*, house or palace (Venetian)
calle: street open at both ends (Venetian)
cambio: exchange; money-changing office
camera: room
campanile: bell tower
campo: literally, field; in Venice, neighborhood square
Carnevale: Carnival. In Venice, the popular annual festival is celebrated for three weeks before Lent, and Venetians playfully don masks and costumes and bid "farewell to meat."
caregha: chair (Venetian)
chiesa: church
ciao: hello; good-bye
coltello: knife
coperto: cover charge; covered
corte: courtyard; court
(a) destra: right (versus left)
enoteca: wine bar
facchino: porter
fondamenta: long, broad street along a canal
francobollo: postage stamp
gettone: pay-phone token
gondola: privately hired sightseeing boat
goto: glass (Venetian)
IVA: value-added tax
libreria: bookstore; for monuments, library

magazzino: ground floor

mezzanino: first floor (above magazzino)

mille grazie: literally, a thousand thanks; thank you very much

monastero: monastery

museo: museum

ombra: literally, shadow; in Venice, a glass of wine, traditionally served in the shadow of the Campanile

osteria: tavern; restaurant

palazzo: building, palace

passeggiata: stroll, walk (noun)

per favore or *per piacere*: please

piano: floor, story (of a building); slowly

piano nobile: main floor

piatto: plate

piron: fork (Venetian)

piscina: in Italian, swimming pool; in Venice, street that was once a canal, a *rio terrà*

ponte: bridge

portacenere: ashtray

ramo: literally, branch; narrow street that opens into a wider one (Venetian)

(Festa del) Redentore: annual religious festival of the Redeemer (Redentore) held on the third weekend of July in Venice

Regata Storica: annual historical regatta held on the first Sunday of September in Venice

rio: canal (Venetian)

rio terrà: canal that has been filled in to make a street

riva: in Italian, shore or bank; in Venice, narrow passageway along a canal

ruga: in Italian, wrinkle; in Venetian, street

rughetta: small street

salizzada: wide street

(Festa della) Salute: annual religious festival held on November 21 in Venice

scalini: stairs

sciopero: strike

scuger: spoon (Venetian); *scugerin*: coffee spoon (Venetian)

scuola: school; in medieval and Renaissance Venice, a charitable community and cultural center set up by a guild

(mi) scusi: excuse me

sestiere: district

(a) sinistra: left (versus right)

sottoportego: entrance to a courtyard, under a building

tovagliolo: napkin

traghetto: ferry; in Venice, public gondola ferry crossing the Grand Canal

trattoria: restaurant

vaporetto: steamboat; in Venice, waterbus

Food and Wine

aceto: vinegar

acqua minerale: mineral water

antipasto: appetizer

Bardolino: light red wine

Bellini: cocktail invented at Harry's Bar, made with champagne or Prosecco and peach juice; named after the family of Venetian artists

branzino: sea bass

calamari: squid

Cabernet: full red wine

Carpaccio: very thin slices of raw beef, served with mayonnaise (or olive oil and lemon) and shaved Parmesan cheese; named after the Venetian artist Vittore Carpaccio

coda di rospo: monkfish

contorno: vegetable course

dolce: dessert; sweet

fegato alla veneziana: Venetian-style calf's liver with onions

filetto di San Pietro: fish fillet (Venetian)

fritto misto: mixed fried fish
gelato: ice cream, only better
granseola: crab
insalata: salad
Merlot: full red wine
olio: oil
pasta e fasioi: pasta and bean soup (Venetian)
pepe: pepper
pesce: fish
Pinot Grigio: white wine
polenta: corn mush, which can be prepared in a variety of ways
primo: first course
Prosecco: light, sparkling wine
risi e bisi: rice and peas, sometimes prepared with onion and ham (Venetian)
risotto: heartily original rice dish, which can be prepared with meat, seafood, or vegetables
sale: salt
scampi: shrimp
secondo: second course
seppie: squid
seppie in nero: squid in black ink sauce
Soave: crisp white wine
spritz: aperitif of wine, liquor, and sparkling water
tiramisù: rich dessert made with sponge cake, cream, coffee, liqueur, and chocolate
Tiziano: a champagne (or Prosecco) cocktail with dark grape juice, named after the Venetian artist Tiziano Vecellio
Tocai: dry white wine
Valpolicella: hearty red wine
vino: wine
zabaglione: creamy dessert made with egg yolks, Marsala, and sugar
zucchero: sugar

HISTORY

Since prehistoric times a scattering of hearty fisher folk lived by the Venetian Lagoon and drew sustenance from its calm and shallow waters. Theirs was a simple and peaceful life among tiny island villages; they were secure in their isolation from mainland danger and oblivious to its consequences.

By about the early fifth century A.D., however, many neighboring mainlanders had had enough. With increasing frequency, Alaric the Goth and his forces swooped down through the peninsula and had their way with Italy: burning cities and villages, plundering what wealth was left, raping and murdering the people.

The city fathers of Roman mainland towns such as Oderzo, Aquileia, and Altino decided to relocate their operations to Malamocco and Jesolo, along the strip of land between the Adriatic and the Lagoon. Later, when they recognized the possibility of attack directly from the sea, they moved to islands within the Lagoon itself, where they found safety from invasion by troops on horseback and by seagoing ships. Eventually, their settlements became the townships of Torcello, Grado, Bibione, Caorle, Heraclea, Murano, Poveglia, Chioggia, Sottomarina, and Rialto.

Legend has it that a nascent form of self-government was officially instituted at noon on Friday, March 25, 421, when diverse communities united under tribunes of appointed officials. These men acted according to directives from Constantinople and looked out for Venetians' better (business) interests.

In 452, Attila the Hun began his sacking of northern Italy. In the years that followed, the Lagoon's asylum villages began to swell from an influx of wealthy refugee families seeking sanctuary there.

The transplanting of landlocked knowledge and wealth proved a boon to the innocent fishermen, who began to realize their potential through new financial

Niche sculpture

power. The resulting business ventures, created in collaboration with the more sophisticated businessmen, expanded their meager food-gathering labors into profit-making enterprises. Soon the Lagoon dwellers were exporting their produce up and down the rivers of Italy and along the Adriatic coast.

Sturdy seagoing ships were built to carry swiftly their perishable produce to an expanding network of ports of call. And on homeward voyages the ships' holds were filled with exotic commodities that further enriched Venetian life: fabrics and spices, precious metals, woods and minerals, household products and implements of work and war. And with these came foreign languages, different customs and religions, and new knowledge and technologies.

Even the ships became marketable commodities. Shipbuilding became another industry within the Lagoon community.

But it was salt that made the Venetians wealthy. Scraped from the edges of evaporating tide pools and packed into barrels stacked high below ships' decks, this most basic of essential compounds proved to be worth twice its weight in gold. And it was on these pylons—fishing, sea trade, shipbuilding, and salt—that the early Venetians built their considerable empire.

In 697, the twelve ruling tribunes were disbanded in favor of a single head of state. Venice elected as doge Paolo Lucio Anafesto; he answered to Constantinople and did his best to hold together a loose assembly of communities under edicts designed to promote better business for all. He was the first in an 1,100-year-long line of 120 doges; the "Most Serene Republic of Venice" represents the longest continuous government ever invented.

Under the stable control of the doge, Venice's businesses thrived. Expanding trade routes required a more formidable navy to protect them, and soon Venetian economic and military forces had mastered the seas.

In 810, Pepin, son of Charlemagne, failed in his attempt to invade Venice. By forcing the consolidation of assets on the Rivo Alto ("high bank") and creating an identity that was uniquely Venetian, he inadvertently unified these communities. Entering the Lagoon with his warships, ready to conquer the resource-rich aquatic city, Pepin was, nevertheless, unclear of where to turn next. So he stopped off at the nearest island, Malamocco, where he discovered a solitary old woman in the abandoned fishing village. He demanded that she reveal the Venetians' whereabouts. *"Sempre diritto,"* she replied, her trembling finger pointed across the quiet water.

Charged with delusions of victory, off Pepin sailed. Right into the Lagoon's entrapping sandbars and shallows, which left him stranded high and dry. Suddenly, in scudded the Venetians with their little flat-bottomed boats; they picked the armada clean in no time at all. (This wouldn't be the last fleet fleeced by the sons of Venezia!)

Venice prospered further from the resulting treaties with Constantinople and gained greater independence from its distant rulers. Immediately the city exercised its newly won power over central Europe and began looking for the religious might to enforce it. In 828, two fishermen—Buono Malamocco and Rustico da Torcello—delivered that holy strength in the form of the body of St. Mark: it had been stolen from Alexandria and spirited away from its Islamic guardians, hidden in a basket covered with pork. A year later, St. Mark became the patron saint of Venice and the first doge's chapel was built in Piazza San Marco to enshrine the body. His symbol—the winged lion—became the symbol of the Republic and the people rallied 'round the flag, fortified with the knowledge that their relic was superior to that of St. Peter's in Rome.

The next three centuries saw an explosion of Venetian expansion across the Mediterranean, Black, and Red seas. Everything it touched, it owned. Everything it wanted, it took. It was the gateway linking Europe with

Africa and Asia. All wealth, all knowledge, all power passed through Venetian hands; and shrewd business-people that the Venetians were, the best of everything seemed to settle in their pockets.

The Crusades of the twelfth century brought even greater business opportunities to the Republic. Remaining neutral throughout, Venice served as the shipping agent for the Holy Wars, carrying European troops and supplies to battle against the infidels; European prisoners to the Islamic counterforces; and always, loot from the conquests of both sides back to the Lagoon. The powers in Constantinople were so outraged by Venice's shameless mercenary activities that in 1171 all 11,000 Venetians who lived within Byzantine walls were arrested and their property confiscated.

That same year, Venice divided itself into six *sestieri*, or districts: Castello, Cannaregio, Dorsoduro, San Marco, San Polo, and Santa Croce. The division was intended to facilitate tax collection in preparation for retaliatory war against their rulers.

At the start of the Fourth Crusade in 1198, the blind doge Enrico Dandalo found himself holding a wad of unpaid bills from the Crusaders' past campaigns; he leveraged this outstanding debt into a most profitable means of revenge against Christian Byzantium. Convincing the Holy Warriors to make a small detour from their rescue of Jerusalem, the old man led an unconscionable attack against Constantinople and brought the Byzantine Empire to its knees in 1202. Of the priceless treasures he pillaged from that great city, the Four Horses of San Marco are the most famous.

With the collapse of the Byzantine Empire in the East and the decline of the Holy Roman Empire in the West, Venice enjoyed an era of prosperity and world domination unlike any other in its history. The fruits of the earth were sweetly Venice's. And Marco Polo's fortunate opening of trade with China in the late thirteenth century provided a delectable icing to their already sumptuous cake. Over the next two centuries, the expanding economy led the way for the massive growth of the Republic itself. The Venetian empire controlled much of the northern Italian mainland, all of the Mediterranean Sea, and the islands of Crete, Rhodes, Corfu, and Cyprus.

But the discovery of the Americas by Christopher Columbus in 1492 and the opening of spice routes to India by Vasco da Gama soon after marked the beginning of a long, slow decline of Venetian maritime supremacy. Its monopoly of global commerce dissolved. The Atlantic became an ocean of opportunity, not "the end of the world," as it was once considered. European consciousness was directed westward, and Spain and Portugal ruled the waters of the Atlantic with new types of wind-powered ships, which left the Venetian man-powered galleys in their wake.

Undaunted, the Venetian ruling class reinvested its fortune inwardly and became a haven for musicians, artists, and architects and an ideal environment for the Renaissance. Operas and concertos, paintings and sculptures, churches and palaces of unparalleled splendor were created. Once again, the world flocked to Venice for inspiration and enrichment; the population grew to 200,000 in the city itself: three times the size of London and Paris combined. And tourism surpassed trade as its major enterprise.

Napoleon envied greatly the riches Venice held, and in 1797, he rolled over the city, declaring, "I shall be an Attila to the state of Venice." And for almost twenty years he was. He executed its leaders, destroyed its churches, carried off its artworks, looted its treasuries—in short, pillaged Venice much as Venice had done to Constantinople six centuries before. Even the Four Horses he carried off to Paris as his personal trophies of victory.

Once he had picked the city clean—and after he had met defeat at Waterloo—Napoleon handed Venice over to the Austrians, who exploited her resources further still. Yet the Venetian spirit of innovation, industriousness, and independence survived. Even after their elected annexation to the recently created Kingdom of Italy in 1866, the natives here considered themselves Venetian first, Italian second—and they still do.

Today Venice stands as a tribute to that spirit, although a little faded and in need of some repair. Nowhere else in this hemisphere can one find history and heritage so richly preserved. Everyone who visits here is handsomely rewarded by the experience and leaves a bit of his heart behind.

Walk · 1

Patriots, Prisoners, and Nuns

TO THE ARSENALE AND BACK

The Campanile

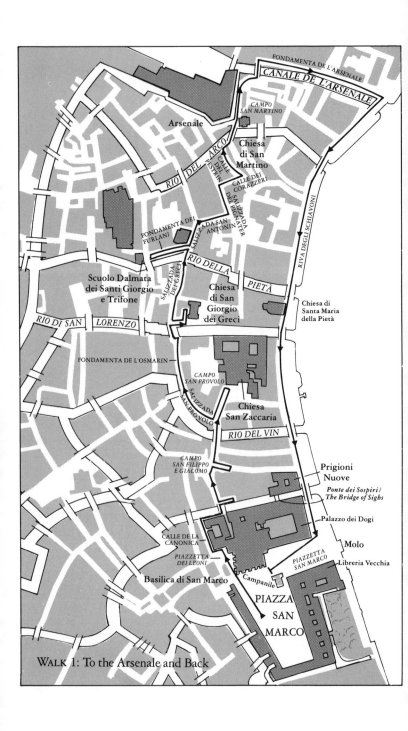

FONDAMENTA DE L'ARSENALE

CANALE DE L'ARSENALE

CAMPO SAN MARTINO

Arsenale

Chiesa di San Martino

RIO DEL ARCO

CALLE DEL PESTRIN

CALLE DEI CORAZZERI

SALIZZADA DEI PIGNATER

RIVA DEGLI SCHIAVONI

SALIZZADA SAN ANTONIN

FONDAMENTA DEI FURLANI

RIO DELLA

SALIZZADA DEI GRECI

PIETÀ

Scuolo Dalmata dei Santi Giorgio e Trifone

Chiesa di San Giorgio dei Greci

Chiesa di Santa Maria della Pietà

RIO DI SAN LORENZO

FONDAMENTA DE L'OSMARIN

CAMPO SAN PROVOLO

SALIZZADA SAN PROVOLO

Chiesa San Zaccaria

RIO DEL VIN

CAMPO SAN FILIPPO E GIACOMO

Prigioni Nuove

Ponte dei Sospiri / The Bridge of Sighs

Palazzo dei Dogi

CALLE DE LA CANONICA

Molo

PIAZZETTA DEI LEONI

PIAZZETTA SAN MARCO

Libreria Vecchia

Basilica di San Marco

Campanile

PIAZZA SAN MARCO

WALK 1: To the Arsenale and Back

Starting Point: Piazza San Marco

This walk is best enjoyed in the morning—between 9:30 and 12:30—to take full advantage of the opening hours of shops, museums, and religious facilities, as well as the relative scarcity of tourists. Plan on taking three hours to complete it.

If you stand in the center of the Piazza and look straight on at the beautiful Basilica di San Marco, you're facing east-northeast. Whether the sky is cloudy or clear, the full morning sun is before you. By the time you reach the farthest point on this walk, you and the sun will have traded places.

No matter where you step here, you do so, quite literally, on the footprints of tens of millions of other visitors. There exist on this earth few such places where so many have come for so long and for so many reasons. Only two others come to mind: Vatican City and Mecca. But theirs are decidedly devotional destinations. There, one goes to revel in Heaven. Here, one comes to revel in Humanity (or at least the humanities).

To place this walk in some historical context: We'll be spanning the late Byzantine and early Renaissance eras of Venetian history. The people and places to which we'll introduce you have come into existence around the time of the discovery of the New World, during the fifteenth and sixteenth centuries.

When Mediterranean-locked Venetian businesses reached their peak of prosperity, the horizons of the rest of the world were dramatically shifted westward across the Atlantic. Venice's ability to partake of New World opportunities was severely limited, as Venetian ships were pinched off at Gibraltar, beyond the city's control. And while sailors along Venetian trade routes only pondered the idea of a New World, Spain and Portugal availed themselves of its wealth.

It was only four years after Columbus's discovery that Gentile Bellini painted his *Corpus Domini Procession* and stood close to where you are now. (Actually, to capture the Piazza in full perspective, he painted the procession from one vantage point and the surroundings from another.) More than two hundred years later, using techniques of even wider scope, Giovanni Antonio Canal, called Canaletto, stood in and around this space and created some of the finest cityscapes in history. (Of course, the Piazza has also inspired "artworks" of more dubious nature. Late in this century, Coca-Cola immortalized its logo by creating it in bird food and letting hungry pigeons spell out the product name!)

We leave the Piazza by way of **Piazzetta dei Leoni,** the courtyard to the left of the Basilica. Immediately there to greet us are two antique lions done in red Verona marble by Giovanni Bonazza in 1722. Their faces are pockmarked and worn away, but their backs have been polished glossy-smooth by innumerable children's squirming bottoms as they sit on them and pose for parents' pictures. Beyond the central wellhead—pigeons crowd its fountain birdbath—in the back right-hand corner of the *piazzetta*, under an arched recess in the side of the Basilica and behind black-bronze gates, we find a **Monument to Daniele Manin** (May 13, 1804–September 22, 1857). He was an avid patriot of Venice and beloved hero of the ill-fated second uprising against Austria in 1848–1849. Even if briefly, his story is worth relating.

The son of a converted Jew, Daniele followed custom

and took the name of his patrician sponsors. As a young lawyer in Venice, his was one of the first voices calling for freedom from Austrian rule and the independence of a united Italy. He was promptly imprisoned by Austrian authorities.

On March 16, 1848, Venetians rebelled against their harsh rulers. They stormed the prisons, freed their favorite son, and carried him outside on their shoulders in celebration. Five days later, Venice succeeded in pushing much of the Austrian army as far back as the fortifications of Verona.

At once a new government was formed, and Manin was named to head the Republic. He would hold the position for less than eighteen months. But at that moment he had more pressing matters to attend to; he led resistance fighters in winning back possession of the Arsenale (shipyard) and the fleet while simultaneously battling to control the strategic railway bridge, which had been opened only two years previously. Badly damaged in the fighting, the railway would not reopen until 1851. (Many of us arrived—and will depart— via these tracks. On the trip out, at about the midpoint in the bridge, remember to look north and note the small island monument erected to honor these warriors.)

Unfortunately, winning these battles would not win the war. Cut off from the rest of the peninsula and besieged by Austrian forces on all sides, Venice vowed "resistance at all costs." The city valiantly endured constant bombardment, starvation, disease, and an ever-dwindling supply of equipment and manpower. Ironically, it was a summertime cholera epidemic that finally broke the back of the freedom fighters. On August 23, 1849, Venice was forced to surrender and to resubmit to the powers of Austria for another seventeen years. Manin and his compatriots were expelled from their homeland and lived out the rest of their days in exile.

Today, a century and a half after Manin's exploits of

idealism and courage, this little-noticed monument stands in quiet remembrance of his noble deeds. Four poetically mourning lions support on their backs a brown stone sarcophagus containing his ashes; a dried, faded laurel wreath lies against it in quiet tribute to a man whose indomitable spirit lives on in the hearts of Venetians.

To our immediate left, forming a right angle with the Basilica, is the white neoclassic façade of the **Palazzo Patriarcale**, looking square and solid. Completed in 1850 after a design by Lorenzo Santi, it is the residence of the bishops of Venice. Since 1492, starting with St. Lorenzo Giustiniani, Venetian bishops have been given the title of patriarch. In this century, three such patriarchs have become pope: Pius X (1903–1914), John XXIII (1958–1963), and John Paul I (1978).

Proceeding to the left of the Palazzo Patriarcale, we continue along the Calle de la Canonica, where a number of little shops display works of lace for sale. If you are in the market for such purchases—and you do not plan an excursion to the enchanting island of Burano, where authentic laceworks are made—you may enjoy window-shopping along the way.

Soon, we reach a canal, Rio del Palazzo, across which stands a fine example of Renaissance architecture: **Palazzo Trevisan**, built in the early sixteenth century. Here lived Bianca Capello, grand duchess of Tuscany, after her marriage to greedy, paranoid, and despotic Grand Duke Francesco de' Medici, in 1578. Legend has it that at dinner on October 18, 1587, Bianca attempted to serve a visiting cardinal (her brother-in-law Ferdinando de' Medici) a poisoned tart. When he insisted that Francesco taste it first, she, too, ate from it and killed herself with the same sweet, *dolce*, thus joining him in the hereafter. *Ah, la dolce morte!*

Today, behind its cracked and weathered stucco façade, which resembles panels of faux marble, showrooms display Murano glassware and give daily demon-

Palazzo Trevisan

strations in the art of glassblowing, once considered a state secret. At one time, in fact, a glassworks artisan lived like a nobleman—his daughters could even marry into the ruling class—but if he ever left the Republic with his knowledge, he was instantly labeled a traitor and condemned to death. His immediate family was imprisoned and Venetian hit men were dispatched to track him down and kill him on the spot. So much for the power of a monopoly.

After turning right onto Fondamenta de la Canonica,

we walk less than three gondola lengths and climb the steps to reach Ponte de la Canonica. From this bridge, we view the back of the two official buildings of the Republic in St. Mark's Square: **Palazzo Ducale** (the Doges' Palace) and the **Cappella di San Marco.**

Standing in the middle of the bridge, facing the greater waters of the Canale di San Marco beyond, we see on the right the huge Renaissance façade covering the Doges' Palace and St. Mark's Basilica. The line of demarcation between the two is visible in the back of the palace, at the point where it was begun around 1300; it was completed two centuries later.

On the left, toward the end of the canal, we have the New Prison, **Prigioni Nuove,** built at the end of the sixteenth century by Antonio da Ponte, who also built the Rialto Bridge at about the same time. The prison was the site of Casanova's legendary escape on October 31, 1756, which he vividly described in the autobiographical *Histoire de ma fuite (Story of My Escape)* in 1788. (The former fiddler, adopted into nobility by a Venetian senator, had been sentenced to five years' confinement for introducing two young noblemen to the practices of Freemasonry and, therefore, revealing secrets against the state. He had served fifteen months when one night he slithered through a hole in the roof of the prison, with a priest named Balbi in tow. Together, they clambered over the eaves to safety and freedom. Shortly thereafter, Casanova hightailed it to Paris; he introduced the lottery to France and became quite wealthy, always continuing his amorous shenanigans.)

Connecting the Prigioni Nuove and the Palazzo Ducale is a suspended bridge on the second floor, the Bridge of the Prison, better known by Byron and his nineteenth-century peers as **Ponte dei Sospiri,** or **Bridge of Sighs.** Built in 1637 by Antonio Contino (nephew of Antonio da Ponte), this Baroque construction in white Istrian stone connected prisoners' cells to the chambers of justice.

One can imagine the poetry of the moment: The

condemned man, manacled and mangled, pauses for an instant and gazes out one of the tiny square windows at the glistening waters of his beautiful and beloved city. And with a sigh he burns the image into his mind: his last look at freedom before being led to a dungeon's dark and dank doom.

Today, a romantic tradition keeps this little canal one of the busiest in all Venice. It is believed that if a married couple ride a gondola—and kiss—under the Bridge of Sighs, their union will last forever. (This was easy to conceive for Italians: Italy allowed no divorce until 1976.)

Looking past the Bridge of Sighs and the ever-crowded Ponte della Paglia beyond and below it, we can see, rising on an island across the great Canale di San Marco, **Basilica di San Giorgio Maggiore**, a beautiful church built by Andrea Palladio in 1580 (Walk 3).

On the other side of the *rio*—at no. 4312—is the entrance to the recently reopened **Museo Diocesano d'Arte Sacra**, the Diocesan Museum of Sacred Art, and the **Chiostro di Sant' Apollonia**, the Cloister of St. Apollonia (open 9:00–12:00 and 15:00–17:00; tel. 5229166).

Built in the twelfth century, this is the only Romanesque cloister in Venice and the best example of Venetian construction of the period: a brick pavement atop pylons; airy double columns and irregular arches; wood between the floors to give flexibility to a structure built on constantly resettling sediment.

This is an example of what much of Venice must have looked like before the great transformation of the Gothic period. Around the cloister are displayed sculptural fragments and stone inscriptions of names and Latin sayings, souvenirs from the original St. Mark's. The cloister was renovated in 1969; photographs show the sorry condition before restoration.

At the far end of Santa Apollonia is the entrance to the Diocesan Museum of Sacred Art. It contains vestments, relics, ceremonial objects, as well as paintings and sculptures from churches permanently closed or unable to ensure the safekeeping of their treasures. Some of us might wish to step inside for a quick look around.

We go back to the Ponte de la Canonica and turn right onto a small street, Rughetta Santa Apollonia, which widens into Campo San Filippo e Giacomo. We take a sharp right around the corner, into the narrow Calle dei Albanesi; there is a little coffee bar on the left, at no. 4237A, called **M. le Bonifacio**. Its sign has been removed from over the door, but you can still make out the name in the stonework. A favorite place among natives, it is busy and filled with animated conversation, and is especially well known for the quality of its fresh pastry.

You may want to try a chocolate-mousse *bignè* or the *zabaglione*, both delicious confections. The cappuccino here is considered by many the best in Venice (and by many Venetians, the best in the world). Two charming young women in blue-gray-and-white-striped uniforms work behind the counter. Bonifacio offers a good opportunity to pause for a moment, enjoy a cup of coffee, chat with the hostesses, eavesdrop on conversations, sample one of the superb little pizzas, *pizzette*, and read a bit ahead in this chapter.

This is a good time for a short digression or two, the first for *caffè*. In Venice, as in all of Italy, coffee can be prepared in many different ways: strong, black *espresso*, served in a small cup (and unlike the frequent Americanized version, *without* a twist of lemon). If you want it stronger still, order it *ristretto*. An *espresso* lightened a bit with milk in a small cup is a *macchiato*. If you'd like a larger cup than you'll get with a *cappuccino*, ask for *caffèlattte* (the milk can be *caldo*, warm, or *freddo*, cold). If you like your coffee *very* light, ask for *latte macchiato*. If you want an American-style coffee, ask for *caffè doppio in tazza grande*. And iced coffee is called *caffè freddo*. Whatever you order, it will be quite good, indeed. Enjoy it at your leisure.

The second digression is a modern-day legend in the making. It's about two brothers who introduced something that is integral to Venetian life today.

Façade of the Doges' Palace

To begin this story, we return to nearby Campo San Filippo e Giacomo. Here, on the left, under the two middle awnings of no. 4338, is a popular restaurant, the **Trattoria Conca d'Oro** (closed Tuesdays; tel. 5229293).

Owned by the Costa family, the restaurant is a busy and boisterous place, renowned for its food and worthy of note and frequent return. Many contend that these friendly folks are the purveyors of the best pasta in Venice; indeed, their *tagliolini alla poareta*, black pasta with rings of calamari, is one of the finest dishes anywhere. Attractively presented on red-and-black plates, the pasta gets its color from the squid ink; the flavorful and memorable sauce is derived from seven types of fish in addition to the calamari. Chef Sergio Salah guards this recipe closely, as well as the recipe for his Sicilian-style fish soup, *zuppa di pesce alla siciliana*, which distinguishes this restaurant above most others. Interestingly, though, it was neither pasta nor soup that gave this family restaurant its start.

In 1947, Giuseppe and Giovanni Costa sailed from Sicily to Venice to seek their fortune. As the young brothers gazed out at the sunset-gilded waters of Palermo bay and the semicircle of land surrounding it—the Conca d'Oro, or Golden Conch—they vowed to honor their family and keep alive the memory of their beloved homeland.

Upon arriving in Venice, they were marked as outsiders; their dress and dialect were as alien to Venetians as the food they were first to offer for sale: pizza. At first, business was slow (Italians are notoriously chauvinistic toward their own regional cuisines, and Venetians possibly more so than most). No one seemed to know what to do with the strange, thin-crusted pies, no matter how good they tasted. Still, the budding restaurateurs persevered, and slowly, they built a loyal neighborhood following.

Then, in 1951, Giuseppe was approached by the owner of a very well-known restaurant in another district; Al Teatro, in Campo San Fantin. (That popular restaurant still stands, next door to Venice's most famous and beautiful theater, La Fenice.) Al Teatro's owner figured that pizzas were good, quick, high-volume, low-overhead fare, especially if served to his always hurried, always hungry after-theater crowd. Would the Costas approve his including pizza on Al Teatro's menu? he asked.

Now until that point, the Costas' pizza monopoly had been a meager one at best, and they wisely realized that popular education was the key to their restaurant's success. "Yes!" they encouraged, "Serve pizza and serve it well. The more people who develop a taste for the pie the better!"

So, with Conca d'Oro's blessing, Al Teatro began a friendly competition, and the rest is history. (If you have the chance, try the *pizza Posillipo*. It's a delicious, light-crusted pie with *frutti di mare*, or seafood: shrimp, mussels, calamari, and chopped clams lightly washed with olive oil. You'll see why pizza has become a staple here, as all over Italy.)

Today, Giovanni runs the place with his two curly-haired sons. Signor Costa is your host; you might recognize him by a shiny gold space-shuttle pin he wears on his lapel: a medal of sorts awarded to him on April 20, 1989, by U.S. astronaut Robert Springer, who rightly declared the food at the Conca d'Oro "out of this world!"

Moving toward the right of the *campo*, we proceed along Salizzada San Provolo to the iron-railed *ponte* spanning Rio del Vin. This small, quiet canal is used mostly as a parking space for gondolas and other small boats; the city issues the necessary permits.

Down from the bridge, we stand in Campo San Provolo, facing a beautiful Gothic archway, surmounted by a late-fifteenth-century sculpture depicting the Madonna and Child, St. John the Baptist, and St. Mark. Bartolomeo Bon was the sculptor, who worked also on the main entrance to the Doges' Palace.

From here, we enter the *campo* of the round-shouldered **Chiesa di San Zaccaria,** the model for many churches throughout the Continent and Great Britain. It's a peaceful square, adorned with a thirteenth-century brick bell tower. The church itself was begun by Antonio Gambello in 1444, in red and white stone and in the Gothic style; it was completed in Renaissance style by Mauro Coducci in 1515. Its façade is one of the earliest examples of large-scale Renaissance architecture in Venice.

The church was once part of the Monastero di San Zaccaria, dedicated to Zacharias, the father of St. John the Baptist, whose remains are said to repose inside the church. Formerly, the monastery was a convent of extremely wealthy, powerful, and rowdy Benedictine nuns.

It was a common practice in medieval Venice for middle-class fathers to send their daughters to convents and thus avoid the burden of a dowry. Needless to say, not all of these young women liked the idea of their lives being so preordained; they did not easily resign themselves to pious chastity and devotional prayer to God.

The Monastero di San Zaccaria proved a real haven for a number of these rebellious and lusty women. Legends still live of how they brazenly entertained lovers at day-long feasts, attended by eager noblemen; a number of illegitimate children were born to the nuns, and blackmail of city rulers became standard business practice. Over time, the convent evolved into a power base of extensive influence, intrigue, and wealth.

Such wealth, in fact, that for a time the nuns owned half of St. Mark's Square. Known then as the Brolo (orchard), it was a vast, grassy tract planted with vines and fruit trees. The nuns deeded it to the city in the twelfth century, and from then until 1797, the doge visited the convent every year at Easter to give thanks to the order of nuns and receive the *corno ducale*, the red ducal cap. This celebration was represented in paintings by Canaletto, who included it in some of the most famous cityscapes of Venice.

The present San Zaccaria is the third church on this site. As we enter, we can see evidence of all three; we will begin looking at the oldest.

For a small fee, you can visit the original crypt to the right of the main hall of the church. (You'll have to ask the attendant to turn on the lights.) Pass through the choir room and descend the stairs to the left. Most of the time, the brick floor of this low-lying nine-vaulted crypt is covered with water. Dating from 890, it is the oldest extant piece of architecture in Venice today. Here is a chance to appreciate how much the level of the rest of the city has risen from its earlier foundations.

When you come out of the crypt, enter the **Cappella di San Tarasio,** one of the most beautiful Gothic chapels in Venice. It was decorated over eight hundred years' time; the floor mosaics around the altar, in Roman style, are from the fourth century. The main section of the building dates from the fifteenth century. The adornment of the chapel was begun in Venetian Gothic style by Giovanni d'Alemagna and Antonio da Murano around 1400–1420.

Frescoes are a rare form of decoration in Venice. Large-scale paint-in-plaster has a tendency to crack and crumble under the stresses of a structure's constant resettling on shifting pylons. But here, the most important and remarkable decorations are the frescoes on the chapel arcade. Executed by Andrea del Castagno in 1442, they represent God the Father, the evangelists, and saints. The condition of the frescoes is extraordinary. Enjoy them even more by using the coin-operated lighting system.

On exiting the chapel, check the glass display case of handicrafts by the nuns: lace, embroidery, printed music books (a Venetian invention in 1511).

We return through the first room in the older section, used as a choir by the nuns. There we see three important paintings: *The Birth of St. John the Baptist*, by Jacopo Tintoretto; *The Escape to Egypt*, by Giovanni Battista Tiepolo; and above the door, *The Crucifixion*, by Leonardo Bassano. The wooden choir stalls (1455–1464) are the work of Francesco and Marco Cozzi; these stalls survive from an earlier Gothic church and were restored in 1595 to be used by the nuns.

The main structure, also known as the "Monastery of Nine Saints," houses not only the remains of St. Zacharias, but the bodies of eight other saints as well. In centuries past, it was believed that holy relics—especially the bodies (or pieces of bodies) of biblical figures and saints—actually enhanced the religious strength of a congregation. Obviously, these sisters really meant business. They were so wealthy they could acquire as many saints as they wanted to increase their prestige and power.

On the wall to the right of the main altar, to the right of the door leading to the crypt, is a small side altar. Here lies the silver-masked body of St. Zacharias, below which lie the remains of St. Athanasius, patriarch of Constantinople.

After the fall of Constantinople, the main structure was built even larger to show that Christianity was not dying. The Gothic architect Antonio Gambello worked on it from 1444 until his death in 1481. Two years later, the Renaissance architect Mauro Coducci took up the assignment; he completed it in 1515. Their two distinct styles are evident throughout.

Directly behind us, to the left of the main altar, hangs a splendid painting by Giovanni Bellini, master of Titian: *The Madonna and Saints*. Be sure to use the coin-operated lighting system for a better look. The painting depicts the Virgin Mary and the Christ Child on a throne, in the company of four saints: Jerome in red, Lucy with a transparent glass bowl, Catherine with grain and plow, and Peter with his key.

Bellini's artwork is more than mere religious representation, it is masterful public relations for the industries of Venice. Lucy's glass bowl represents the crystal artistry of Murano; Peter and Jerome hold books, recalling the Venetian printing industry. At the Virgin's feet, an angel plays a musical instrument, yet another product of Venetian manufacture. All are dressed in beautifully embroidered clothing imported from around the world by Venice's merchants.

The most remarkable aspect of this painting is its vivid three-dimensionality. Recent restoration has unveiled Bellini's use of light and color. The dramatic depth of field is accomplished by a number of techniques, not the least of which is Bellini's deliberate reproduction, in the background, of the marble columns that frame the painting. The white-and-red marble floor in the painting reflected the chapel's actual flooring, now since replaced. (One can, however, see the same pattern in the floor to the left and right.)

What Bellini creates, then, is an all-engulfing environment. The viewer is part of the setting and is drawn into it; he is not just an observer but a participant.

This seemingly tranquil painting was a declaration of war against the still current but dying Gothic style. Before this, representations of happiness, beauty—even health— were not considered viable in man's earthly life. His role was to suffer and become worthy of beauty in the hereafter. One can imagine that Bellini's revolutionary depiction of the holy grouping may have been considered almost sacrilegious to masters of schools of flat-and-somber art.

Nevertheless, in 1506, during his second visit to Venice, the German master artist Albrecht Dürer declared this painting the most beautiful on earth. Unfortunately, it was mutilated by Napoleon, who cut off the top when he removed it from the city in 1797. After the defeat of the Little Corsican at Waterloo in 1815, many of the paintings he had stolen were returned to the rightful owners. Luckily, this was one prize that came home to Venice.

Other noteworthy pieces of art in San Zaccaria include sculpted works by Alessandro Vittoria (who is buried in the church). The most remarkable of these is the statue of St. John the Baptist on the holy-water stoup to the right of the entrance.

After exiting the church, we go back under the archway and return to Campo San Provolo. Turn right, walk under the *sottoportego* and through Calle San Provolo, where, at no. 4719A, a quaint little shop produces some of the finest masks—in leather and pressed paper, *cartapesta*—for Venetian Carnevale. The leather works are really quite extraordinary and worthy of a collector's attention.

On the left, at the end of Calle San Provolo and the beginning of Fondamenta de l'Osmarin, is a lovely *capitello* with a silver-crowned Virgin Mary and Child. This shrine is believed to protect the people who live on the street. Look for the daily offerings of flowers made by residents to honor their protector.

On the inside left, at the corner formed with Rio di San Severo, stands the Gothic **Palazzo Priuli** with its precious little garden. Once the residence of a family of merchants, it is representative of a life-style enjoyed in the fourteenth and fifteenth centuries, when the wealth of trade expanded the city's size and scope.

Each floor in the palace served a different function.

The ground floor—characterized by small windows with iron bars—held the merchant's wares. Even the heaviest of merchandise floated easily in and out when high tide flooded the rooms. Above that, the *mezzanino* housed the offices. Ceilings were kept low (*mezzo* means "half") for easy heating in winter. Next up, the *piano nobile* was the showplace of the home, lavishly decorated with chandeliers and original works of art. Here the family displayed its wealth and entertained guests with concerts, plays, banquets, and balls. Finally, the fourth level was the actual family residence. The building was meant to accommodate forty to fifty people: family, office workers, and servants; in the back, a small additional level served as quarters for the hired help. An impressive edifice, for a family of appreciable wealth and influence.

To the right of Palazzo Priuli is Devil's Bridge, **Ponte del Diavolo,** so called because it once connected a convent and a monastery and was responsible for numerous dangerous liaisons between amorous nuns and monks. One is not surprised to hear that the passageway was also called the "Bridge of Temptation."

Mary McCarthy, in *Venice Observed*, informs us that Venice reserved a special punishment for philandering priests in the fifteenth and sixteenth centuries: they were hung in a cage known as a *cheba*, which was suspended by a pole out of the middle window of the Campanile in Piazza San Marco. One poor soul spent an entire year in such a cage, to the morbid amusement of Venetians and visitors alike.

Continue to the bridge at the end of the *fondamenta*, Ponte dei Greci, which spans Rio di San Lorenzo, named after the martyred saint. Crossing the *rio* over right-angle bridges, we enter the area of the city historically given to its Greek population, whose influence and importance to the empire of Venice cannot be understated.

Between 1200 and 1676, Venetian rule had reached down the coast of Yugoslavia, across Greece, and as far as Corfu, Crete, Rhodes, and Cyprus. More than 450 years of political domination and interaction through trade and cultural exchange melded Venetian and Greek societies inextricably. Especially after the fall of Constantinople in 1453, Greek culture and traditions continued most strongly in the Greek community in Venice.

The result of this can be seen today in this area's architectural heritage. Immediately to our right is the **Collegio Flangini,** home of the Istituto Ellenico (no. 3410–2), a center of Hellenic studies (open 9:00–12:30 and 13:30–17:00; closed Tuesdays). Enter through the tall black iron gates, built by Baldassare Longhena in 1678, who also built Santa Maria della Salute, the stunning basilica across the Grand Canal from the Hotel Gritti Palace that is so effectively lit at night (Walk 3).

Inside the courtyard, we find a church, **San Giorgio dei Greci.** It was built in 1541 by Santo Lombardo, but the dome was not completed until thirty years later. San Giorgio combines Renaissance architecture with Byzantine iconography. Inside, the iconostasis covers an entire wall; through its three doors pass the priests—and only the priests. There are many paintings here, two of which are special: a twelfth- or thirteenth-century Byzantine Madonna and early-fourteenth-century Christ Pantocrator, both brought to Venice before the fall of Constantinople.

At the time, this area became an important center of Greek culture, including the Orthodox religion. Still today, San Giorgio serves the Orthodox community, which remains a vital element in Venetian society.

Outside, on the right of the church, is a lovely courtyard with a white stone well decorated with the scene of St. George killing the dragon. This courtyard is one of the most peaceful and least visited sites in Venice. Take a minute and appreciate its autumnal cool silence, the smell of springtime blossoms on the trees, or the summer song of swallows darting overhead.

Towering overhead nearby is the *campanile* (1587–1592); it competes with the tower of Pisa because it leans off plumb as the supporting pylons continue to sink into the sediment.

As we exit, on the right are the **Scuola di San Nicolò dei Greci** and the **Museo d'Arte Bizantina**, in a building designed by Baldassare Longhena in 1678. Today this museum of Byzantine art displays icons and a good collection of works by Byzantine artists from Crete, dating from the fifteenth through the eighteenth century.

Exiting the complex, we turn right on Calle de la Madonna and reach Salizzada dei Greci. At the beginning, at no. 3416, we find a fine, small, family-owned Venetian restaurant, **Trattoria Da Remigio**, which specializes in seafood. The mother works the kitchen; the son is the waiter; and the father makes drinks behind the counter. You may be welcomed like a long-lost relative. The *spaghettini con i capperozzoli*, thin pasta with double-necked-clam sauce, is recommended. This spot is very popular among natives and it is therefore advisable to call in advance for reservations (closed Tuesdays, tel. 5230089).

At the end of the street, cross the canal, Rio della Pietà, at Ponte San Antonin. Before noon, this canal is always busy with boats delivering huge bottles of wine, fresh produce, and other restaurant supplies. Turn left onto Fondamenta dei Furlani and end at the **Scuola Dalmata dei Santi Giorgio e Trifone**, the School of Saint George of the Dalmatians (open 9:30–12:30 and 15:30–18:30; closed Mondays). A visit here is one of the most rewarding half-hours that can be spent in Venice.

As Venetian world influence grew throughout its history, so too did the city become increasingly cosmopolitan. Numerous ethnic groups came and settled here in specific neighborhoods, bringing with them their customs, traditions, and languages. To foster these various backgrounds and interests (and as a means of identifying and controlling them), the city established six major schools, *scuole grandi*, each representing a community's heritage. In time, the centers of learning diversified further into more than two hundred minor schools, *scuole minori*, catering to fraternities of artisans, craftsmen, scholars, musicians, and other professionals.

Most of the *scuole* were of a charitable nature; they

fed and clothed the needy, and sponsored and supported orphanages and hospitals. Many included orders of religious zealots—flagellants, actually—who on holy days would move through the city in long processions, quite literally whipping themselves into a frenzy.

From 1000 to about 1800, the Republic of Venice controlled Dalmatia, a region in what is today Yugoslavia; an important part of the city's population hailed from there. The Scuola Dalmata dei Santi Giorgio e Trifone, founded in 1451, is the only *scuola minore* still functioning today; it is run by the Knights of Malta, as a museum and community center.

Set into the small Renaissance façade of the *scuola*, which dates from the middle of the sixteenth century, is another representation of St. George skewering the dragon. This powerful and important image is seen throughout Venice, and especially in this district. Push aside the brown curtain fluttering in the breeze; a surprise of white light will flood the dimly lit interior.

Inside, we find one of the most beautiful and untouched art treasures in all of Venice. From 1502–1508, the interior was decorated with paintings by Vittore Carpaccio, who, with Giovanni Bellini, was a reigning artist of his time. The interior is one of the most evocative of early Renaissance art. The walls of the small main room are entirely decorated with paintings relating to the lives of three Dalmatian peasant saints: Jerome, Tryphone, and George.

Starting from the left wall, we have the painting depicting St. George killing the dragon, an impressive and particularly gruesome representation of the saint's symbolic victory over the evil infidels. After the fall of Constantinople to the Turks in 1453, the symbolism of St. George, whose triumph represented the hoped-for victory of Christianity over Islam, became more pronounced. In the middle of the background of the painting, a tree divides the work into two parts. It has leaves—and therefore lives—on the side of St. George, while it is barren—dead—on the side of the monster.

Interesting, too, is the precise moment captured in the painting. In a scene littered with corpses and body parts—perhaps a more realistic portrayal of the Holy Wars than most bargained for—the painting freezes the instant in which the dragon is impaled. The weapon shatters on impact. It has served its purpose; the monster is dead; the war is over; St. George will fight no more. Hundreds of years later, Gustave Moreau and Salvador Dalí borrowed and reinterpreted Carpaccio's symbolism in their own works.

The next painting on the left, *The Triumph of St. George*, is dominated by an enormous Renaissance building representing a new type of architecture and the new philosophy of life, emerging from the Age of Rebirth.

On the left of the end wall, St. Tryphone baptizes the Gentiles, permission to do so being his reward from the grateful king for the rescue of his daughter. The altarpiece is a Madonna and Child by Benedetto Carpaccio, son of Vittore. Finally, we see the miracle of St. Tryphone. In the background is an imaginary vision of Venice with bridges, canals, and a palace prepared for celebration; carpets are displayed from the windows, much as is the current practice on holidays. Even if this scene is invented, it predates by five hundred years the reality of Venice today.

On the right wall are *The Agony in the Garden* and *The Calling of St. Matthew*, which is depicted taking place in the Ghetto, the Jewish district, of Venice. Again, this is an idealized work.

The last three paintings deal with St. Jerome. The first depicts the saint leading a lion into a monastery; in the background is the *scuola* itself before the new façade was erected. Next is *The Funeral of St. Jerome*. And the last painting, directly opposite St. George killing the dragon, is of St. Augustine in his study, entranced by a vision of St. Jerome's death. The painting gives us an idea of the interests and life-style of the new type of man emerging from the Renaissance. We see the study of an enlightened intellectual surrounded by instruments of music, science, and astronomy. He is no longer a man of war but one of research, contemplation, and understanding.

Upon exiting the building, retrace Fondamenta dei Furlani and take Salizzada San Antonin, where birds in cages sing in the sun from windows overhead. You will pass the eerie, black, one-eyed door of the fish store at no. 3490; unfortunately, its claw knocker is frozen in place and can no longer be used.

Turn left on Salizzada del Pignater and then right before the **Trattoria ai Corazzieri,** a good place to stop for lunch. This little, out-of-the-way restaurant, comparatively devoid of tourists, has tables outside on the Corte dei Preti.

Here's a chance to sit and stare out at the easy daily life unfolding around you: an old woman hanging laundry out of a window, young mothers filling buckets at the central water fountain while their children play soccer across the pavement, men returning home for the midday meal and filling the space with conversations about the soccer standings. . . .

When a Venetian tells us he loves Venice, he does not refer to Piazza San Marco and its bustling commerciality. He talks instead of places like this, where the pace of life slows to match that of a stroller, where one is reminded that the true simple pleasures of life are found right under one's nose.

A kindly, middle-aged waiter once worked the tables outside the *trattoria.* His older, very jealous, companion lived in an apartment across the way, overlooking Corte dei Preti. Every time the gentleman waiter dawdled over conversation with his customers, the older man would fling open the shutters and hurl insults out the window. This would touch off a comic display of gestures and words between the two men and an assortment of good-natured jokes from the neighbors. Sometimes these scenes would happen every half-hour or so; they always ended with the slamming of shutters left rattling in the breeze. All the waiter could do was shrug and smile in understanding. "His memory is gone," he would explain, "but I love him for loving me so much."

When you continue with your walk, the narrow alleyway you will enter is Calle dei Corazzeri. (You won't see the sign until you are at the other end, where you turn left onto Calle del Pestrin.) As you reach Rio del Arco, and before crossing over the little iron bridge, glance in the door just to its right. Here is a workshop for gondola tools, the *laboratorio* **Spazio Legno.** Quite likely, you will be invited inside for a closer look.

In a tradition from the Middle Ages, the family of craftsmen here custom-carves the long oars and distinctive oarlocks, *forcole,* which are hand-fashioned to individual gondoliers' tastes, dimensions, and requirements. It's quite amazing to hear a gondolier talk about the tools of his trade. Each man thinks of them as lifelong friends, members of his family. "She's the most beautiful *forcola* in all of Venice!" one brags. "This oar belonged to my grandfather," another states proudly. "Someday it will be my son's. And his son's after him."

In a similar father-to-son tradition, the oars are fashioned of laminated beechwood; the *forcole* of single pieces of walnut. These objects are made for work and in model form for artistic decoration. The Museum of Modern Art in New York City has a number of *forcole* in its permanent collection.

After crossing the bridge, we reach Campo San Martino. The **Chiesa di San Martino,** built by Jacopo Sansovino in 1550, appears to keep its own irregular hours and may very well be closed, but peer through the iron-grated-and-glass doors at its lovely interior before proceeding farther. Note, if you can, its awe-inspiring painted ceiling, which seems to open up to a heavenly vista.

Moving along the *rio* to the **Arsenale,** you approach the farthest point on this walk.

From this facility, started in 1104, the world learned the word *arsenal* (from the Arabic *dar sina'ah,* "house of

Forcole

industry"). And for five of the last eight centuries, the Arsenale remained the symbol of Venetian military and technological superiority. It was in operation until the end of World War I.

With the revolutionary innovations of assembly-line and interchangeable-parts manufacturing (predating Henry Ford by some eight hundred years), the Arsenale's workforce of 16,000 produced up to a hundred battleships per month. Dante was so impressed with the site that he borrowed and adapted the scene in the eighth circle of his *Inferno*.

The secrets of Venice's dominant galley-building industry are still guarded by fortification. Under naval authority today, the area is officially off limits to the casual visitor (although the no. 5 *vaporetto* goes through it via the canal); we can, nevertheless, appreciate the imposing gateway barring our entrance.

The gateway, in the form of a triumphal arch, was constructed in 1460, the first example of Renaissance architecture in Venice. Atop the archway stands a winged lion, the emblem of St. Mark and of the Venetian empire. In his claws he holds a book. Usually, it is open and inscribed, in Latin, "Peace be unto thee, Mark, my evangelist." But here the tome is ominously closed, symbolizing that this place means business and its business is war; the important, deadly secrets of warfare are held firmly within. Higher still is a statue of St. Giustina, another patron saint of Venice, and the dominant saint of the Venetian victory over the Turks at the Battle of Lepanto on October 7, 1571.

In front of the gateway are four huge Greek lions brought from different parts of the Venetian Republic. The one on the left came from Piraeus harbor in Athens, by Doge Francesco Morosini, whose true infamy came when he blew up the Parthenon because the Turks were using it to store gunpowder. The graffito in Old Scandinavian carved into this lion's back was recently attributed to an eleventh-century Norwegian mercenary fighting in the Mediterranean. It reads: "Haakon, together with Ulf, Asmund, and Worn, conquered this port." One should note that young Haakon (a.k.a. Harald) later became king of Norway. No doubt his penchant for self-promotion served him well.

Across the wooden bridge, after turning right on Fondamenta de l'Arsenal, you reach Riva degli Schiavoni; a waterfront stroll will bring you back to Piazza San Marco.

Immediately on the left is the entrance to the **Museo Storico Navale,** the Naval Museum, housed in what once was the naval granary. Lovers of ships and naval warfare should visit here at their leisure. The museum has an impressive assortment of armaments, ship models, and maps (open 9:00–13:00; Saturdays 9:00–12:00; closed Sundays).

Time permitting, you may want to detour farther, to the **Paradiso** restaurant and its scenic views of the water. The Public Gardens, **Giardini Pubblici,** are a few steps beyond and provide a rare opportunity to walk among lush greenery in Venice. And—if it is in summer of an even-numbered year—you may wish to attend the **Biennale** to view the international exhibition of modern art.

Jenny Holzer, from Hoosick, New York, famous for her aphoristic sayings on billboards and T-shirts, and one of the country's most visible contemporary artists, was selected to represent the United States here in 1990 and won the pavilion prize. She is the first woman to hold this honor, and she joins an impressive roster of American artists. Among them are the late sculptor Isamu Noguchi and the painter Jasper Johns, whose works were exhibited here in 1986 and 1988 respectively. Johns, incidentally, won the Biennale's grand prize in 1988; within days of the announcement of the award, on November 9, 1988, his painting *White Flag* was auctioned at Christie's for $7 million, the highest price ever paid for a work by a living artist. Twenty-four hours later, at Sotheby's, his *False Start* sold for $17 million. Obviously, winning the Biennale can have a significant impact on an artist's life.

If you want to head home, turn right. Along the way, you'll pass the **Chiesa di Santa Maria della Pietà,** originally a school where orphan girls were taught music. The present building was erected to celebrate one of the greatest musicians of all time: Antonio Vivaldi, "the redheaded priest," who was a master there from 1703 to 1745.

Directly across the Canale di San Marco, we see the stately **Basilica di San Giorgio Maggiore,** one of Andrea Palladio's greatest achievements (Walk 3). A visit to the church, which sits on its own island, is highly recommended, especially for the magnificent views of Venice from its *campanile*. To the right is **Giudecca** island; to the left, in the distance, is **Lido** island, another highly recommendable site for visit, exploration, and relaxation on its breezy, cabana-lined beaches lapped by the gentle Adriatic. (It's only a fifteen-minute ride away on the *vaporetto* no. 34.) The Lido is also the home of the summer casino and the Venice Film Festival.

This is the busiest expanse of water in Venice. Hydroplanes zip in and out, to and from Yugoslavia; cruise liners moor here for their passengers' day trips into the city; *vaporetti, motoscafi,* tugboats, barges, ferries, waterbuses, watertaxis, and pleasure boats of all kinds move through the harbor at all hours, miraculously avoiding the tiny gondolas out for hire.

Practically every *vaporetto* stops along Riva degli Schiavoni to take you anywhere in the city. You might consider taking the no. 5 *circolare*—Venice's version of New York City's Circle Line—on its hour-plus, very scenic circumnavigation of Venice proper. (The ride can be particularly pretty at night.) You would also take it to reach Fondamenta Nuove, from which you hop a boat to Murano, Torcello, Burano, and the other outlying islands.

We approach—and pass—an impressive stone-and-bronze monument with beautiful representations of winged lions, *leoni,* among which real cats, *gatti,* play and sleep in the sun. Already we wade among a sea of tourists and souvenir vendors, but we press on.

Soon we pass the **Danieli,** considered by most to be the finest hotel in all of Venice. It was once Palazzo Dandolo (where the first opera was performed in Venice, in the early seventeenth century: Claudio Monteverdi's *Proserpina Rapita*) until its commercial conversion in 1822. Eleven years later, George Sand and Alfred de Musset occupied room 10, seeking—but not finding, according to the hotel's brochure—"their dream of absolute, true and complete love." (In *Venice for Pleasure,* J. G. Links tells us that Musset renounced his love for his mistress on the first night and skipped off to the slums of Venice to revel in debauchery while Sand seduced a young doctor whom she later took along to Paris only to discard.) Charles Dickens lived in a corner suite in 1844 and returned to the same rooms in 1853. The brilliantly opinionated and sadly impotent John Ruskin lived in room 32 in 1849 and 1850 while working on his immortal *Stones of Venice*. And George Eliot and George Henry Lewes checked in here on June 4, 1860.

A century and a quarter after the Danieli's opening, an addition to it replaced a collection of ramshackle wooden huts and stalls that for seven hundred years had filled the space between it and the Doges' Palace. This mini-slum was actually ordered into existence by the Republic after Doge Vitale Michiel I was murdered on the site in 1102 and his assassin hid out in a stone building; he was later captured and hanged for his crimes. Wanting to prevent any similar occurrences in the future, the government destroyed the stone building and forbade any permanent construction to take its place. The Danieli management, however, presented a more financially rewarding and architecturally pleasing solution to the problem.

Next we have the entrance to the **Prigioni Nuove**, the New Prison, which we saw from behind at the start of the walk. You may want to tour the building and visit one of the cells where prisoners' names and laments have been scrawled on the walls. And where, some say, Lord Byron spent two days carving them deeper into the stone to preserve them for all eternity.

This gloomy seventeenth-century structure was brought into being after the decline of the Venetian warship industry. The Republic had always manned its galleys with those convicted of crimes against the state; the punishment was more akin to slavery than rehabilitation. But as the demand for Venetian-style warfare and ships diminished, the city's overflowing courtrooms needed a place in which to incarcerate and punish their criminals. The prison was used continuously by four governments:

first by the Republic of Venice, then by the Napoleonic Empire, then by the Austrians, and finally by the government of Italy. Tragically, it remained in operation as late as 1922.

Until recently, there lived in Venice a woman who was born in the Prigioni Nuove. Her father had been a political prisoner; her mother, having nowhere else to live on her own, joined him. Their baby spent her childhood within these walls, learned what she knew from cellmates coming and going, and until the day she died, spoke in a Venetian dialect unique to herself. One can only wonder at the scene when she first stepped outside and into freedom.

If you tour this place and creep through its dreary cells, you might consider this sobering thought as well: Conditions inside here now are better than those of most prisons around the world today. Admittedly, humanity still has a long way to go; luckily, we on this walk do not.

When crossing the bridge, Ponte de la Paglia, look to the right for a reverse-angle view of the **Bridge of Sighs (Ponte dei Sospiri)**. In the corner of the Doges' Palace to the left, we see a fifteenth-century stone carving depicting the Drunkenness of Noah.

After descending the bridge, we enter the waterfront area before Piazzetta San Marco, traditionally known as the **Molo** (pier). To our right, we see the original façade of the **Doges' Palace**; this façade was designed by Filippo Calendario, who was executed for treason in 1355 (Walk 4). An independent tour of the palace is strongly recommended.

In front of us rise two huge Anatolian granite columns. (Legend has it that a third, irrecoverably lost while it was being unloaded, lies at the bottom of the Lagoon.) The columns were stolen from Syria and presented to the city by Doge Domenico Michiel in the early twelfth century. It took the engineering skills of Nicola Starantonio, the builder of the first (wooden) Rialto Bridge, to raise them. For his triumph, Starantonio was awarded Venice's first gambling concession, which he operated between the columns themselves for many years.

More than mere "triumphal erections," these pillars formed the site of many a political execution, and the victims' bodies were left dangling in the wind from them for days at a time—a grotesque welcome-and-warning to visitors. In 1609, in *The Totall Discourse of the Rare Adventures and Painful Peregrinations of Long Nineteen Years*, William Lithgow wrote of his arrival at the Molo. As he stepped off the gangplank, he looked up to witness the roasting of a Franciscan friar, "for begetting fifteen young Noble Nunnes with child all in one year—he being also their father-confessor."

Atop one column rises a statue of St. Theodore astride a crocodile (or whatever it is). The work was probably a Roman portrait statue, brought to Venice as loot, identified as the city's (then) patron saint, and given this place of honor. This particular statue is a reproduction replacing the original. And the Greek soldier St. Theodore was "replaced" by St. Mark in 829 as the real religious power of the Republic.

Atop the other column—although it was still under restoration and therefore absent at the time of this writing—the real symbol of Venice stands in all its glory: the winged lion of St. Mark and the Republic of Venice. This creature probably started out as a chimera in Assyria or China, and—as with other spoils of war—the Venetians quickly adapted the image to their own purposes and have sanctified it ever since.

We walk between the columns and enter **Piazzetta San Marco.** Photographers snap pictures of sightseers covered with pigeons; salesmen hawk postcards, posters, and miniature versions of gondoliers' hats; and all over the place people bump into one another and ask for directions.

To our left stands the **Libreria Vecchia,** the Old Library, built by the architect Jacopo Tatti ("Sansovino") to

Atop the Libreria Vecchia

house the Biblioteca Marciana, a collection of nine hundred Greek and Latin manuscripts bequeathed to the Republic by Cardinal Bessarion; another extensive collection of books that once belonged to Petrarch was meant to be housed here as well, but it was lost in storage and never recovered. (The library contains a copy of every book printed in the Venetian Republic during the sixteenth and seventeenth centuries.) One might venture inside to see the impressive reading room, where the library's 1.2 million volumes are accessed.

Ten years into its construction, on December 18, 1545, a portion of the Old Library's vaulted ceiling suddenly caved in, and—just as suddenly—Sansovino was clapped into jail for his mistake. Only through the pleading of his friends, the writer Pietro Aretino and Titian, was Sansovino released and allowed to repair his work (at his own expense, of course). Twenty-five years later Sansovino died, leaving the project still uncompleted. Vincenzo Scamozzi finished the task in 1582; he continued the arches to the corner and added an additional story in the process.

Just ahead on the left, an inevitable line of visitors waits to take the elevator to the top of the **Campanile,** whose bell, the Marangona, rings out at sunup, noon, sundown, and midnight, its peals sending the pigeons into a frantic flutter. The view from the bell tower is truly the finest in all of Venice, especially in the late afternoon, when the sun sets the golden mosaics of St. Mark's all aglow. (The more ambitious of us may wish to scale the tower by means of its internal spiral ramp; in centuries past, frivolous Venetian nobility used to ride horses up to the top.)

This is the second bell tower to stand on this site. The original—which looked exactly like its present-day replacement—was begun in 888 but not completed until 1514, when Bartolomeo Bon capped it with a stone spire and a golden angel weathervane. In its time it was used as a lighthouse, watchtower, and astronomical observatory. It was from here that Galileo Galilei first demonstrated his wondrous telescope in 1609.

Here it stood, through a thousand years' worth of storms and earthquakes, when, with a groan and a shudder, it cracked and collapsed at 9:52 on Bastille Day, July 14, 1902. Amazingly, no one was injured and only the little Loggetta attached to it (where people today buy their tickets and enter the tower) was completely destroyed. Happily, too, Sansovino's beautiful bronze statues escaped harm. Using the actual stones from the first tower, the present one was constructed *com'era, dov'era*—"as it was, where it was"—and opened in 1912.

Around the corner, in the tower wall facing Piazza San Marco, is a small piece of white marble set just a bit above waist-high. The hash mark in it records the highest point reached by floodwaters during the disaster of November 4, 1966. *Acqua alta*, high water, is a common occurrence in Venice. It is not unusual to visit the quiet Piazza San Marco late at night during a full moon and see the pavement ashimmer with a thin washing from the Lagoon.

Indeed, Venetians are always ready to lay out elevated wooden walkways to help visitors and themselves over the high water. But on the days leading up to November 4, 1966, all the elements seemed to conspire against Venice: a full moon, storms at sea, heavy rains, and particularly strong winds from the east and south, the *scirocco*, prevented the tides from receding. Just imagine what this place must have looked like on that winter-cold day!

Since then, a cooperative international effort has tried to find a technological solution to the problem of *acqua alta*. Someday, it is hoped, movable dikes will be installed at the Lagoon's three openings to the sea. When not needed, these massive structures will be filled with water and sunk to the bottom to keep the shipping lanes clear. When Venice is threatened by high seas, the dikes will be filled with air and floated up into service. In October 1988, a working prototype—named *Mosè*, Moses—was anchored in place and successfully tested. (As of this writing, rumors are flying around Venice that this multibillion-dollar public-works project, one of the largest in the world, is about to be canceled.)

We all know that Mother Nature eventually reclaims what is hers. Perhaps our grandchildren's grandchildren will hear of Venice much as we today hear of the legendary Atlantis. And family pictures, stories, and memories will help keep Venice alive.

But for now, let us celebrate Venice's survival and the completion of this first walk. Wade out to the middle of the Piazza—which Napoleon once called the finest drawing room in Europe—and listen to the competing orchestras: one from **Florian** (Europe's first coffeehouse; it served its first cup in 1683), the others from **Quadri** across the way or **Lavena,** where Wagner used to sit composing his music. (All of the orchestras are probably playing back-to-back-to-back renditions of "New York, New York.")

Refreshments at these establishments are, of course,

overpriced, but no visit to Venice is complete without the experience. Each site provides a nice vantage point from which to watch fellow visitors celebrate Venice in their own ways. During the Austrian occupation, Venetians frequented Florian and left Quadri to their conquerors; you can take your pick, help yourself, and have a seat.

Walk·2

Merchants, Explorers,
and Painters

ACROSS PONTE RIALTO

TO SAN ROCCO

WALK 2: Across
Ponte Rialto to San Rocco

Starting Point: Piazza San Marco

This walk requires about three hours to complete. It is best taken between 8:30 and 12:30 or 15:30 and 18:30. It leads you quickly from the crowds and moves you into the day's longer light. If a morning itinerary is chosen, you must pace it to reach Santa Maria dei Frari by 11:00; if an afternoon itinerary is preferred, plan on reaching the Frari by 17:00.

Facing St. Mark's Basilica as we did to start Walk 1, we again gaze out on visitors, vendors, and Venetians. It's hard to imagine this scene otherwise. But indeed, over the centuries, this site has changed its appearance many times and in many ways.

Where we now stand, on a solid stone pavement atop millions of pylons, there once grew an orchard, herb garden, and vineyard, tended by the nuns of San Zaccaria (Walk 1). A canal once flowed across here. The original pavement was made of brick in 1264; the stonework underfoot today was completed in 1735. And the geometric designs of white stone embedded herein served more than decorative purposes; the rectangles and squares defined the sites of market stalls run by the various craftsmen's guilds of yesteryear.

Today, with a few notable exceptions, we will visit the people and places that came into being primarily during the fifteenth and sixteenth centuries, when Venetian wealth from world trade reached its peak and the visual arts grew in prominence and economic importance. This was a time of great change within Venetian society, and the art and architecture created during this era reflected those philosophical transformations. As an example of this, Piazza San Marco is a good place from which to start.

To the right are the **Procuratie Nuove,** the new residences of the nine procurators of Venice, once the Republic's highest governmental officials. Vincenzo Scamozzi began the Procuratie in 1584, drawing his inspiration from Jacopo Sansovino's Libreria Vecchia right around the corner. The new construction altered the entire shape of the Piazza. What had been a rectangular space (approximately 574 by 186 feet, or 175 by 56.6 meters, wide) became trapezoidal, with the Basilica end opening wider (to 269 feet, or 82 meters). During Napoleon's reign, the Procuratie Nuove served as his royal palace, the Palazzo Reale.

Directly behind us once stood the Chiesa di San Geminiano, also by Sansovino. But when Napoleon moved into town, he razed it to construct the Napoleonic Wing, **Ala Napoleonica.** The Little General had wanted to complete his "drawing room" with a series of arches, and he hired Giuseppe Soli, who finished the job in 1807. (He also wanted to demolish every tax-exempt structure he could, to create more money-making real estate. During his short reign, Napoleon destroyed 165 churches and monasteries in Venice.) Across the top of this building, note the string of statues commemorating the emperors of Rome. The blank space in the middle was reserved for a statue of Napoleon himself; not surprisingly, today no one feels much of a need to fill it.

Within the Ala Napoleonica you will find the **Museo Correr** (open 10:00–16:00; Sundays 10:00–12:30; closed Tuesdays). The museum is named after Teodoro Correr (1750–1830), an avid collector of art who left his priceless treasures to the state. In so doing, he helped create one of the two great museums in Venice (the other being the Accademia). The first floor houses displays of historical documents, ceremonial vestments, and currency. Upstairs is a fine collection of works by such masters as Jacopo, Gentile, and Giovanni Bellini and Vittore Carpaccio. In front of the staircase to the entrance of the museum, in the floor under the arcades, is a marble representation of San Geminiano, the church that Napoleon destroyed.

To the left of the Basilica stand the **Procuratie Vecchie**, first built in 1204 and reconstructed by Mauro Coducci after a fire in 1512. Here was the original residence of the procurators of Venice; but when their needs grew too large for the chambers, their residences were moved across the Piazza after Vincenzo Scamozzi razed the Orseolo hospice there to build the Procuratie Nuove. Today, above ground-floor shops and restaurants, the building houses government and insurance company offices.

But now it's time to leave this busy place and proceed along our walk. We will exit through one of the Piazza's many arches.

To a right-handed counter, it's the 105th arch of those surrounding. To a lefty, it's the first. The big one. The Arco dell'Orologio, the arch supporting the **Torre dell'Orologio**, so-called Moors' Clock Tower, just before Piazzetta dei Leoni. Since 1502, the clock has set Venetians' sense of their place amid time and space.

The central part of the clock tower was built between 1496 and 1499 by Mauro Coducci, easily the most important architect at that time in Venice. (He also built the façade of San Zaccaria, which we visited on Walk 1.) The wings, possibly by Pietro Lombardo, were added between 1500 and 1506. The set-back upper floors were added by Giorgio Massari around 1755. The structure complements nicely the Basilica nearby, with its bright enamels and intricate statuary.

The gilt-and-enamel clock face marks the hours,

phases of the moon, and relation of the sun to the zodiacal signs. The massive and intricate mechanism was devised by G. Paolo Ranieri and his son G. Carlo, who labored for three years to perfect the clockworks. When they'd done so, legend has it, the Republic had both men blinded so that no other city could ever have such a magnificent timepiece. Apparently, the government's brutal precautions worked; for generations, this remained one of the most precise clocks on earth. (Unfortunately, a few years ago the old man in charge of maintaining the mechanism died, and the city has been unable to find anyone willing to take up the task of mastering the mechanics. As a consequence, after each day's winding, the clock's accuracy ticks away by the minute.)

Just above the clock face is a little terrace on the mezzanine floor. Here sits a Virgin Mary (in gilded beaten copper by the sculptor and goldsmith Alessandro Leopardi), holding the Christ Child on her knee. During Ascension Week, a parade of religious figures marks the passing of each hour. A trumpeting angel leads the way for the three Magi; each bows to the Mother and Child as he passes before them.

Above this, before a background of rich blue mosaic and dozens of golden eight-pointed stars, stands sternly the winged lion of St. Mark, whose left forepaw holds open the tome to its sacred blessing of peace on one and all: *"Pax tibi Marce."* For a number of years, a statue of Doge Agostino Barbarigo (1486–1501) knelt in homage before this lion; the figure was removed in 1797.

Inside the archway, on the left at no. 147, is a small door that leads to an internal stairway. From here, you can climb the clock tower to the rooftop terrace for a close-up view of the internal workings of the clock and the Moors striking the hour. At the time of this writing, the staircase is under restoration and therefore inaccessible. These muscular figures, by the way, are called Mori, Moors, because of their dark patina. They were cast of gunmetal at the Arsenale in 1494 by Ambrosio de la Anchore and, as Guilio Lorenzetti points out, probably from models by Paolo Savin.

Exit the piazza through the archway under the clock tower and proceed along **Mercerie** (or **Marzaria**) **dell'Orologio,** the main street of Venice, which gets its name from the haberdasheries *(mercerie)* that once lined it (nowadays it seems sellers of sunglasses have taken over). Always crowded by day, it's the busiest shopping street in town. And it's a good, direct route to the Rialto. Never mind the jostling, you will be away from the crowds soon enough.

It was on this street, on a rainy Monday—June 15, 1310, the Feast of St. Vitus—that a legendary accident took place. At that time, Doge Pietro Gradenigo sat as figurehead of the government, and an unpopular one he was. Under his rule, Venice had become embroiled in a dangerous feud with the pope over biblical interpretation; the pope excommunicated the Republic and those who resided there. Almost overnight, all of Venice found itself confronting spiritual and financial ruin by this isolation from the outside world. And Gradenigo became the most detested man on two legs. The time was ripe for revolution.

His rival Baiamonte Tiepolo returned from self-imposed exile on the mainland and managed to assemble a sizable force of like-minded malcontents around him. And on that rainy Monday, they attempted to stage a coup d'état. Tiepolo led the angry crowds toward Piazza San Marco with a hearty standard-bearer at his side. Under the banner's single-word rallying cry, *Libertas,* the mob shouted slogans of revolt and aroused the curiosity of a poor old woman, Giustina Rossi, who came to her window to see what was going on. Leaning on the windowsill, she knocked over a piece of marble, which fell to the pavement, hitting the standard-bearer on the head and killing him outright.

This was an ominous omen. Suddenly, the once boisterous revolutionaries panicked and disbanded in chaos, dashing to the ground Tiepolo's hopes of governmental reform. As Gradenigo's troops moved in and mopped up the mess, Tiepolo retreated across the Rialto Bridge and burned it in his wake. In due time, however, he was captured and exiled for his crimes against the state.

In remembrance of this event, just past the clock tower, at the Sottoportego del Cappello, is a commemorative relief called *The Old Woman with a Brick*. And below that, set in the street pavement, is a small white stone that marks the spot where the stone fell.

Proceed along this street until you cannot go straight any longer, and take what will be your third right. Just ahead, you'll find the **Chiesa di San Giuliano,** known in Venetian dialect as **San Zulian.** Back in the middle of the sixteenth century—at about the midpoint of the Renaissance—a scholarly and eccentric doctor named Tommaso Rangone sponsored Jacopo Sansovino's renovation of this charming little church.

Some thirty years before, the Florentine architect, whose reputation rivaled Michelangelo's, had fled the Sack of Rome. And like the original settlers of the Venetian Lagoon, he sought sanctuary on the Rialto. His name preceded him and quickly he became the official architect of the Republic. By 1554, he had chalked up a number of admirable designing credits, the Libreria Vecchia and Palazzo Ducale (Walk 1) among them.

During the renovation of the façade of San Giuliano, a mishap occurred that recalls the catastrophe visited on him during the construction of the Libreria Vecchia: the roof caved in. This time, instead of being locked up in prison, Sansovino was teamed with Alessandro Vittoria, a protégé of Andrea Palladio and the sculptor who completed the decorations of the Doges' Palace; together, they were charged with the complete reconstruction of the church.

In honor of their understanding and generous benefactor, Sansovino created a bronze portrait statue of Dr. Rangone and placed it over the front door. (The kindly

Venice's symbol, the winged lion of St. Mark

doctor later became a best-selling author when he published a book on how to live to be 120 years old. Not surprisingly, book sales dropped off after the doctor dropped off at the age of eighty.)

Today, this church is an age-darkened and tired-looking place, but step inside anyway. (Be mindful of the inner glass-and-wood doors. They are rickety and can rattle noisily with each opening and closing.)

Here Venetians come to meditate and pray before a simple red-draped altar, beneath an inspiring ceiling of carved and gilded wood and massive oil paintings. Paolo Veronese's painting of Christ at the Last Supper hangs on the right-hand wall, and a carved-wood crucifix nearby is strikingly lovely. Take a moment and appreciate this little oasis of calm before reentering the bustle outside.

Exit the church, turn right and then right again. Cross Campiello San Zulian diagonally (you may wish to look into the little shop selling masks and dolls). Bear right and cross Ponte de la Malvasia. Follow Calle de la Malvasia. At its end, we find **Casa Canaletto,** the House of Canaletto. In its study, the painter created the most important Venetian landscapes of all time.

Born on October 18, 1697, in San Lio near Ponte Rialto, Giovanni Antonio Canal was the son of a famous theatrical-set painter, Bernardo Canal. From his father, Canaletto learned the techniques of color, perspective, and visual composition.

In his youth, he studied in Rome; by his early twenties he was back in Venice, where he pioneered the art of *vedute,* or view paintings, for which he became so famous. His many paintings of the Grand Canal and Piazza San Marco are marvels of his innovative style; his eye proved the original wide-angle lens.

Unlike many artists of his time, Canaletto steered away from traditional religious representations and focused on vast scenes of everyday Venetian life. His heroes were neither saints nor political personages, but housewives, laborers, boatmen, children, and casual passersby. His paintings became "postcards" of Venice and found a successful market especially in England, where he lived from 1746 to 1755. The largest collection of Canaletto's work is owned by Britain's royal family.

If you continue in the same direction as before, after passing a small courtyard and walking under a *sottoportego,* you will arrive at Salizzada di San Lio. Turn left and enter the *campo* of the **Chiesa di San Lio.** Nowadays, this area is known more for its shopping and sandwiches than anything else.

The church honors Pope Leo X, who served the Church in this capacity from 1513 to 1521. At the time, the Holy Roman Empire and the Republic of Venice were (yet again) at serious odds with each other in religious matters. Pope Leo favored the Venetian point of view and Venice, naturally, favored him.

The church underwent continuous transformation for a period of about seven hundred years, from the late

eleventh century to 1783, when it achieved its present
form. Inside are two important artworks. The monochrome ceiling fresco showing St. Leo in glory with angels
and Virtues is by Gian Domenico Tiepolo, son of Giovanni Battista Tiepolo, one of the greatest artists in
eighteenth-century Europe. (The father-and-son team
worked all over Europe; their last commission was in the
royal palace in Madrid.) The second treasure can be
found at the second altar on the left: a work by Titian
depicting apostle James (1540–1550). A mature work of
the master, it is currently under a sorely needed restoration to bring back its complex and vivid color.

Exit the church through its main doors and pass under a mournful keystone face. Continue to the right along
Calle Carminati. As you pass under the tangle of old wis-
teria, look into the busy printing shop. (They do fine
work here; no doubt you've already seen many of their
posters around town.) Cross Ponte del Pistor, also known
as Ponte delle Paste. On the bridge itself, on the left, you
will find **Rudatis,** a very good pastry shop. Specialties
here are small éclairs called *mignon* and very good coffee.

Proceed along Calle del Pistor. Make a quick left, then
a right at Calle Malvasian. Here you might well be greeted
by a family of all-white cats in Corte del Forner. Pass the
wellhead, and turn left onto Calle Scaleta. The shop at
the end on the right, **Gabbiani,** sells exquisite perfume
bottles and vases (open 10:30–12:30 and 16:30–19:45;
closed Monday mornings; tel. 87874 or 703143). Cross
Ponte del Teatro o Marco Polo, pass under the *sottoportego* and enter **Corte Seconda del Milion,** site of the
boyhood home of Marco Polo (1254–1324).

By mid-morning, the little space is bathed in sunlight
and songbirds twitter all around. Maybe a mother's voice
can be heard from an open window overhead. Maybe a
child sings softly to himself. Maybe, standing in this same
spot seven hundred years ago, we could have heard the
song sung by young Marco himself.

Once again, we are surrounded by arches. And in

them, we have a chance to see four hundred years' worth of architectural evolution: from Byzantine to Venetian Gothic.

The large carved-marble arch in the corner shows eleventh-century influence. (John Ruskin obsessed over this arch: he visited many times, taking precise measurements and fretting over the pressure on the arch from above.) It is the last remaining vestige of Marco Polo's home.

Running our hands over its surface, pondering its design, our touch matches Polo's. Perhaps our thoughts do, too. And for a moment, we reach back and touch a life worthy of marvel. Maybe we should take the time to sit on the nearby wellhead and read a little about him.

His father was Nicolò Polo, an upstanding member of thirteenth-century Venetian merchant aristocracy. He formed a partnership with two brothers, Marco and Maffeo, and the Polo trade routes crisscrossed central and eastern Asia and created a prosperous and enlightened life-style for his family back home.

Shortly after the younger Marco's birth, his uncle Marco moved to Constantinople, and the family's scope of operations widened considerably. Nicolò and Maffeo traveled regularly between Venice and the Byzantine capital—sometimes as far away as the Crimea—and their stories filled the boy with an eagerness to follow in his father's footsteps.

By 1260, the senior Polos had made their way as far east as Bukhara, where they chanced to meet an envoy returning from a mission for the Mongol ruler, Kublai Khan. They joined the caravan and ventured back through Cathay to the Great Khan's court in what is now Beijing.

These were the first Europeans the Khan had met, and their tales from such distant lands delighted him and fueled his voracious intellectual curiosity. Deeply interested in the ways of Westerners—particularly their Christian religion—the Khan sent the Polos back to Europe with specific requests of Pope Clement IV. It was his desire that the Vatican dispatch a retinue of scholars to instruct his people in Christianity and the liberal arts.

By 1269, the Polo brothers had reached Acre, where they learned of Pope Clement's recent death. No new pope had yet been elected, and the Polos decided to return to Venice the following year to await the papal appointment. Ten years' absence from home had brought about significant changes in Nicolò's home life; his wife had died and young Marco had grown almost to manhood.

In 1271, the Polos were finally able to fulfill their mission to the new pope, Gregory X, a personal friend of the family's. Shortly thereafter, Nicolò and Maffeo headed back to eastern Asia, bringing Marco with them. For four years they trekked through Persia, over the Ural Mountains and across the Gobi Desert in Mongolia; eventually they reached the Khan's summer palace in Shangtu. By then, twenty-one-year-old Marco had become fluent in the Khan's language and familiar with the customs of his people; he was an immediate favorite of the emperor, who devoted many long days and nights to listening to the young man's tales from his journey. Wisely, the Khan took Marco into his imperial service.

As one of the empire's most trusted officials, Marco traveled extensively throughout the Khan's domain, governing remote cities and conducting special missions into southern India. For sixteen years, Marco, his father, and his uncle served the Khan; they grew extremely wealthy in the process and increasingly invaluable to the emperor's governmental operations. So invaluable, in fact, that he refused to let them depart for home.

Finally, in 1292, the Polos found a way out. An escort was needed for a Mongol princess, promised in marriage to Arghun of Persia, Kublai Khan's grand-nephew. The Venetians were the right men for the job; they packed up for the long haul and spent three years accomplishing their mission. Only then were they allowed to return home.

Wellhead in Corte Seconda del Milion

The Polos' reemergence in Venice is the stuff of legend. Quietly, almost feebly, three tattered beggars appeared in Piazza San Marco. No one, not even their family, recognized them. Then, suddenly, the three Polos ripped off their disguises and opened the linings of their outer garments; thousands of emeralds, rubies, diamonds, and pearls poured down around their feet. Instantly, they became the talk of the town.

And talk they did. Marco's stories of his exploits streaked through the Republic and all of Europe, but most Venetians considered these tall tales, incredible. He quickly earned the nickname "Marco Milione," because he was thought to speak in exaggerations and fantasy. Whether he was believed or not, Venetians were not stopped from entering into quite rewarding trade ventures with the Polos and their allies in China.

These were anxious times in Venice. In the years leading up to 1298, Genoa had risen in power and had begun openly challenging Venice's control of the sea. Amid reports of an impending attack on its shipping lanes, Venice assembled its armada. Marco served as *sopracomito*, or gentleman commander, of one 250-man galley. And on September 6, 1298, off the island of Curzola, the Venetian and Genoese navies clashed, with Genoa the victor. Marco was captured and imprisoned, and he spent the rest of war cooling his heels in the Genoese jail with a cellmate named Rustichello da Pisa.

It seems old Rustichello was an ambitious hack writer with a good ear and a better memory; he recorded Marco's many tales just as he heard them, and after his and Marco's release from prison, he published them under the title *Il Milione*. It is from this book that we today know the accuracy of Marco's powers of observation, analysis, and narration. He was the first traveler to traverse all of Asia longitudinally; the first to describe the court at Beijing; the first to explore China and its borders; the first to describe what are now Tibet, Myanmar, Laos, Thailand, Cochin China, Japan, Java, and Sumatra; the only one in medieval times to mention Zanzibar and Madagascar; and the first European to write of dogsleds, white bears, and reindeer in the far north.

Christopher Columbus owned a Latin version of Polo's book, and in the margins of many pages are notes in the admiral's own handwriting. Clearly, Marco Polo's life helped expand human knowledge across every hemisphere, across New World and Old.

Little else is known of Marco Polo; no real likeness of the man exists (although a representation of him appears on the 1,000-lire note, and a sculpture of him in the Museo Correr depicts him as a top-hatted Chinese gentleman).

Polo's last will and testament, dated January 9, 1324, is kept in the Biblioteca Marciana. In it, he mentions his wife, Donata, and three daughters, Fantina, Bellala, and Moreta. The document was witnessed by a priest and a notary; Polo died the same day they affixed their seals. According to his wishes, his body was interred in the Chiesa di San Lorenzo. Unfortunately, his sarcophagus was lost when the church was rebuilt in 1592.

Perhaps it is appropriate that no physical trace of Marco Polo remains, because his legacy transcends the fortune he bequeathed his family and friends. It is his remarkable spirit that remains with us today, one of open-mindedness, curiosity, courage, intelligence, and worldly wisdom.

On the courtyard wall directly opposite the great arch, surrounding the sign naming the court, we find a series of arches dating to the thirteenth century. To the perpendicular left of the great arch is a set of small windows that are a typical example of fourteenth-century northern Gothic style, the same style as in France, England, and Germany at the time. Directly above the thirteenth-century arches is a series of triple-lobed windows, typical of fifteenth-century Venetian Gothic style, the same style in which the Doges' Palace was decorated and which became the ideological representation of Venice. Another beautiful example can be found just to the perpendicular right, on the *piano nobile*. To find out more about these arches (and all arches, for that matter), read John Ruskin's *The Stones of Venice*, where he describes their stylistic evolution in intricate detail.

Duck through Sottoportego e Corte Prima del Milion and out through the other *sottoportego* (watch your head). Here you will find two restaurants; **Ostaria al Milion** is recommended. It's where local businesspeople eat lunch, so the atmosphere is authentically lively. The food is wholesome, unpretentious, and reasonably priced; service is friendly, efficient, and undoting. *Spaghetti con frutti di mare* is a favorite: pasta, *al dente*, tossed with olive oil, herbs, and an abundant assortment of shrimp, mussels, lobster, and calamari. *Insalata mista*, a mixed salad with arugula, shredded carrots, lettuce, and tomatoes, easily complements the meal. The bread is airy with a smoothly crisp crust; the house white wine is good and dry; the olive oil, in copper pitchers, is light and flavorful. Bad artwork hangs on the walls; the red-and-white-checked tablecloths are worn with use. It's a good place to spend a lunch hour-and-a-half.

A few yards away, you'll find the **Chiesa San Giovanni Grisostomo** (open 11:00–18:15). Its name—also spelled "Crisostomo"—is that of a Patriarch of Constantinople, St. John Chrysostom.

In 1497, a merchant family commissioned Mauro Coducci—of Moors' Clock Tower fame—to replace a smaller church on the site with their own private chapel. Completed in 1507, it was Coducci's last work. It is one of the least well known and most special places in Venice. And in its own little way, this church embodies the religious revolution of Constantinople itself; it is built on the design of the Greek cross.

The Yugoslavian-born St. Jerome translated the Bible into Latin in the fifth century. In the sixth century, Venice chose the Greek version over the Latin and separated from the Church of Rome. The Republic became a renegade state, much like Protestant England later.

Inside the church is a portrait of the saint by Sebastiano del Piombo which dates to 1509–1511. It was commissioned by Catarina Contarini Morosini, who is buried within the church. Notice, on the left of the painting, a group of women dressed in sixteenth-century finery.

Inside the chapel on the right, we see an altarpiece by Giovanni Bellini depicting Sts. Christopher, Louis, and

Jerome. This last saint translates his Bible surrounded by a beautiful landscape evocative of works by Giorgione, whose *Tempesta*, his finest example, is on display in the Accademia (Walk 3). This is Bellini's last painting, described by John Ruskin as "among the most perfect in the world."

In the chapel opposite are marble panels by Tullio Lombardo representing the Coronation of the Virgin, sculpted around 1500–1502. The work was commissioned by a family of rich silk traders. Before exiting, stop before the beautiful, soothing marble bust of a star-haloed Mary in a gold-mosaic niche: the Madonna delle Grazie. Many people pay their respects to this lovely lady every day.

After leaving the church, we follow the "Rialto" signs and cross Ponte de l'Olio. Just ahead, on the right, pass through the post office doors to the **Fondaco dei Tedeschi.** Built with public funds in 1508, it replaced an original structure destroyed by fire, and housed the warehouse, offices, and hostel of German merchants in the city.

Originally, the building's façade was decorated with frescoes by Giorgione and Titian. Some fragments of these frescoes can be seen in the galleries of the Ca' d'Oro (Walk 4), the most notable of which is a naked Venus by Giorgione. On the wall facing the Rialto Bridge, high above the central lion-crowned door, Titian completed his first work, which depicted Judith and Holofernes. Only the faintest trace of it remains.

The Fondaco dei Tedeschi is one of the most important examples of Renaissance architecture created for private use, and it serves as an excellent model of how a business center was organized and run. The ground floor was a warehouse for the merchandise of the various businesses whose offices were right above. The next level had conference rooms and "executive suites." The top floor housed the German tradesmen themselves. All very efficient and self-contained: this suited the Venetians quite

A raft of gondolas

well, since they liked to keep a watchful eye on their foreign partner-competitors.

In this series of arches-upon-arches-upon-arches, we see a new style of constructive design that evolved from the Venetian Gothic after the year 1500. Its effect on architecture can be seen in this century with its influence on Art Deco of the 1920s and 1930s.

Today, this building is the communications center of Venice. Here the visitor can buy postage stamps and send and receive mail, money wires, telegrams, and faxes. There are public telephones as well. If you need such services, now might be a good time to avail yourself of them.

We exit right and turn right again. In a matter of steps, we come to **Ponte Rialto**, the bridge whose name derives from *rivo alto*, meaning "high riverbank." This was the area of Venice first to be settled when the out-islanders consolidated their forces to ward off Pepin's attack in 810 (see "History," page 33). It was and is the chief financial district of the city.

This bridge is the fourth to span the Canal Grande on this site. The first was little more than a floating wooden walkway over barges. Completed around 1180 as one of the original toll bridges, it was called the Quartarolo, after the small coin it cost to cross it. The second bridge was built on pilings in 1264 (the same year Piazza San Marco received its first pavement). In 1310, Baiamonte Tiepolo burned it to cover his retreat from Doge Pietro Gradenigo's troops after Tiepolo's mortar-aborted insurrection against the Republic. This second bridge was repaired well enough to be used for another 140 years; it collapsed under the weight of spectators greeting Emperor Frederick III of Austria in 1450.

The third bridge, again made of wood and this time with a central drawbridge, is depicted in Carpaccio's *The Miracle of the True Cross* (1494), which was originally painted for the Scuola Grande di San Giovanni Evangelista and today hangs in the Accademia.

The present bridge was built of stone on 12,000 pylons in 1591, after a long and heated competition for its design contract. Among the numerous entries were presentations by Palladio and Sansovino. (Palladio's top-heavy, multiarched design—as depicted by Canaletto for his English patron Joseph Smith—was eventually built in Bath two centuries later.) Many contend that Michelangelo vied for the contract as well, but there is no real proof to this claim; the date of the competition does not even correspond to the time Michelangelo was known to have been in Venice (Walk 3).

Sixty years after the selection process began—and well after the masters had passed away—a lesser known (and appropriately named) architect, Antonio da Ponte, was awarded the contract. Recently before this, he had gained favor among the city fathers for his renovations in the Doges' Palace, and his sweeping single-arch bridge design promised to be the most accommodating to the Grand Canal's ever-increasing traffic problems. It also proved a major—and expensive—engineering challenge.

The actual cost of the construction is recorded at 245,537 ducats: a significant amount of money even today. The gold ducat, weighing 3.53 grams, was a highly valued standard of currency throughout the known world. Nearly a quarter of a million ducats weighed in at, roughly, 867 kilograms, or 1,900 pounds: almost a ton of gold. Or about $10 million by today's standards.

But for all its expense, no one, then or now, considers this bridge an architectural masterpiece. It's a stodgy thing, assembled almost crudely and without artistic inspiration; even Rubini's bas-relief side decorations depicting the Annunciation (1590) appear merely adequate at best. The Ponte Rialto is, however, an efficient form that follows its traditional function.

When Shakespeare's Shylock in *The Merchant of Venice* asks, "What news on the Rialto?" he refers equally to the bridge and the immediate neighborhoods it connects. Here, on the banks of the Canal Grande, the world's first financial banks were created (actually, at one time there were some 220 private and public banks). Here, on the bridge itself, the bordering shops lent money and traded in gold and other precious commodities. Here contracts were negotiated, signed, and recorded; partnerships were established; and countless fortunes were won and lost every day for more than six hundred years.

In modern times, the bridge supports a burgeoning retail tourist industry. From morning till night, the little shops hawk souvenirs, keepsakes, and collectibles of all types. Merchandise here is generally of quick-sale nature, although some jewelry, masks, and leather goods of high value and reasonable price can be found sprinkled among the rest. For the most part, lace products are accurately advertised as made *a mano*, by hand; they just happen to be Taiwanese hands and not those of the women of Burano.

Standing at the crest of the bridge, we gaze in either direction from beneath high arches and watch a manic and motley flotilla pass by. As with Piazza San Marco, it seems all people in Venice cross this site at least twice a day. Most probably do. We'll cross it now, possibly try a piece of fresh coconut from a fruit stand's fountain display, and proceed along Ruga dei Oresi and Ruga dei Spezieri. In this area, on nearby Calle delle Sicurtà, the insurance industry was invented to help protect investors in their risky trading ventures around the world.

For many visitors, a detour to the right—through the fish market, the **Mercato del Pesce al Minuto**—can be a sensuous experience. Nearly every weekday from four in the morning to one in the afternoon, this market beside the Canal is crammed with the colors, smells, forms, and textures of every sort of fresh-caught fare. The voices of workers, housewives, chefs, fishermen, and merchants rise in chorus as they haggle over prices and gossip over news. It's a good opportunity to photograph native Venetians in their daily routine.

Cross Parochia San Silvestro and Ponte de le Becarie, named for the *beccheri*, butchers, who worked in surrounding slaughterhouses and meat markets. Squeeze through Calle de le Becarie, enter Sottoportego de la Scrimia, and turn left past the fountain, and then right, to arrive at the tenth-century **Chiesa di San Cassiano** (open 9:30 or 11:30–19:00).

Inside, it is cool and quiet amid columns covered in gold and maroon. There are numerous artworks on display, but only a brief visit is recommended to meet three examples of Jacopo Tintoretto's painting: *The Resurrection with Sts. Cassiano and Cecilia* (1565), *The Descent into Hell* (1567), and *The Crucifixion* (1568), which is one of Tintoretto's masterpieces. At the end of this walk—in the Scuola di San Rocco—we will see a vast collection of the artist's work presented in all its glory.

Back outside, pass just to the left of the little print shop and cross Ponte Giovanni Andrea de la Croce o de la Malvasia. Go through Sottoportego de Siora Bettina and turn left onto Calle de la Regina. Take the next right on

Corte Rota

Ramo de la Regina, pass the sweet-smelling bakery, and cross over Ponte Santa Maria Mater Domini. Enter Campo Santa Maria Mater Domini, with its little shops for iron-work (at no. 2175), silver goods (at no. 2171), and frames (at no. 2178A). Take a short right and walk along Calle de la Chiesa; in a matter of steps, you will reach the **Chiesa di Santa Maria Mater Domini.**

Completed around 1539 with the help of Jacopo Sansovino, the church is newly reopened after extensive renovation was completed in 1989. For those wishing to appreciate yet another work by Tintoretto, his powerful *Invention of the Cross* hangs above the transept. And a very nice Last Supper by lesser known Bonifazio Pitati hangs above the door.

Exit to the right; proceed along Calle Longa, past picturesque Corte Rota on the right with its rare outdoor frescoes. Pass the fur shop on the left at no. 2156 (where, for many years, they've displayed posters of Sylvester Stallone sporting an uncharacteristic full-length mink coat and a cowboy hat). Cross the iron bridge, Ponte del Forner, with its little shrine to St. Augustine on the right. Enter Sestiere di San Polo on Calle del Cristo. Take the next right under the arch, through the Campiello del Forner, under the *sottoportego* and turn left on Rio Terà Secondo. Follow this to Campo San Agostin, walk past it, and follow Calle de la Chiesa.

Cross Ponte de Ca' Donà. Proceed along Calle de Ca' Donà and enter Campo San Stin. Look right and follow the yellow signs to the **Scuola Grande di San Giovanni Evangelista**. This "major school," named for St. John the Evangelist, was founded in 1349 by a confraternity of flagellants, who on holidays were known to walk in long religious processions, whipping their bare backs with rods and spraying the spectators with blood, to their morbid amusement.

The courtyard here is by far one of the finest examples of fifteenth-century Venetian Renaissance style. The entrance gates and architecture of the *scuola* live on as a superb collaboration between Mauro Coducci and the Lombardo family, headed by Pietro: the best melding of the ideals of an architect and the artistic talents of a family of sculptors.

The eagle atop the entryway is the symbol of the St. John the Evangelist. The statue of a woman kneels in homage to him while in prayer to the bronze cross above. In the chapel of this *scuola* is housed the "True Cross,"

Above the gates of the Scuola Grande
di San Giovanni Evangelista

the one responsible for the miracle depicted in Carpaccio's 1494 painting that hangs today in the Accademia (Walk 3). (While being carried in a religious procession, the cross accidentally fell into the Grand Canal and sank out of sight. Then, miraculously, it raised itself out of the water and was recovered.)

If anyone's hungry, by the way, we'd like to make a small digression from this walk and offer a very pleasant recommendation. Quite near here, at the end of the street, you'll find the **Caffè Orientale** (closed Mondays), one of the finest restaurants in Venice. Famous for its traditional cooking, the establishment is owned and operated by the Scarpa family, who are proud to provide their customers the experience of authentic Venetian cuisine. Sandro Scarpa is the host: a congenial and engaging man with a wealth of stories and anecdotes to offer up at the slightest provocation. Be prepared to listen to a litany of daily specials and suggestions as you order your meal; smart customers take his advice. Specialties here include all types of fish; a hearty rice dish, *risotto*; and the traditional custardlike dessert, *tiramisù*. During the warmer months, a small *terrazzo* overlooking a canal is opened for al fresco dining. Nothing is more Venetian than enjoying a leisurely lunch or supper beside the water as gondoliers float by and serenade you with song. A bottle of white wine, *vino bianco*, is always placed just within the boatmen's reach. Many stop by for the refreshment and—still standing on board in their rowing position—toast the restaurant's customers with a happy *"Salute!"*

To get back to our walk: Turn right upon exiting the gateway of the *scuola*, backtrack to Rio Terà San Tomà. Turn left and cross Ponte San Stin and then the next arched white stone bridge at the right (built by the Friars in 1428) to reach the imposing **Basilica di Santa Maria Gloriosa dei Frari,** often called simply the Frari (open 9:30–12:00 and 14:30–18:00, Sundays and holidays 14:30–18:00).

The fall of Constantinople to the Venetians in 1204

brought about a migration of religious orders to the conquering Republic and shifted the capital of Christianity back on Italian soil (see "History," page 35). Venice, naturally, grew in religious influence, becoming a magnet for many forms of Catholicism and rivaling Rome in power.

Two years before the arrival of Saint Francis of Assisi in Venice, in 1222, small bands of his followers (in this case, preceders) began trickling into the city. They were an austere and simple lot, who preached their gospel, performed charitable functions, and begged for their sustenance and shelter. Their life-style of poverty and piety greatly impressed the mercenary and materialistic Venetians, and their hosts took these Franciscan friars, *frari*, kindly to heart.

In 1236, Doge Jacopo Tiepolo donated this plot of land to their order, and a modest little chapel was erected. Fourteen years later, a second, larger church was built, which was used at least until 1333, when the structure we see here was begun in Gothic style (the plan, based on the Latin cross, is attributed to the friar Scipione Bon, who is buried inside).

At the same time, the Dominicans were building their Basilica dei Santi Giovanni e Paolo across town, and an interdenominational competition ensued. All modesty aside, the Franciscans would be *damned* if they'd let the Dominicans construct a larger church! What resulted over the next century was the creation of the two largest Gothic structures in Venice (we'll visit the other, the Basilica dei Santi Giovanni e Paolo, in Walk 4). The Frari was consecrated on May 27, 1542, but not elevated to the status of basilica until February 1, 1926, by Pope Pius XI.

So large were these churches that they chagrined the city government: How could two such massive edifices *not* be political in nature? (As we'll learn at the start of Walk 3, even St. Mark's was a political edifice.) The ruling bodies resolved this dilemma by decreeing that both churches would house the tombs of the doges and other important figures in Venetian history.

Reflecting the Franciscans' philosophical ideal of poverty, the Frari has a simple, sparse, utilitarian brick exterior. However, that belies the fact that the interior houses the world's most extensive collection of art ever created for a single place. And of the many artists whose works are represented here, one is clearly the most celebrated: Titian, the greatest painter of Venetian High Renaissance.

Tiziano Vecellio was born in the alpine village of Pieve di Cadore sometime around 1490. His ancestors had distinguished themselves with military and judicial careers. Apparently, young Tiziano showed early promise as an artist; he was sent to Venice to study painting at the age of nine. First he was apprenticed to Sebastiano Zuccato, then to Gentile Bellini, then Giovanni Bellini, and finally came under the employ of Giorgione ("Big George"), who immediately put him to work on the exterior frescoes of the Fondaco dei Tedeschi. A strong and lasting friendship developed between the two men; when Giorgione died in 1510, Titian completed several of his master's paintings.

It was the death of Giovanni Bellini in 1516 that had the most lasting effect on the artist, however. Titian was immediately named to replace Bellini as the official painter of the Republic of Venice: he held this position of considerable power greedily throughout the rest of his life.

That same year, Titian was commissioned to execute the dominant artwork over the main altar inside the Frari, which we will visit now. The stunning *Assumption*, which was unveiled in March two years later, after many trials and tribulations, is the only painting Titian ever finished on schedule.

After entering the church and paying a modest admission fee, we turn left and confront a vibrant, crimson-clad Virgin Mary as she rises toward her heavenly reward (the vivid red is uniquely Titian's). And as we approach her along the central aisle, through the marble choir screen (built in 1475) and between the beautiful 124-

stall, wooden choir (built by Marco and Francesco Cozzi in 1468, and still in its original position), we soon understand the origin of the old adage "Michelangelo for form, Titian for color."

And just as quickly, we understand why the somber and sedate friars could have been so averse to Titian's work. Shocked by his radical use of color, they fought him tooth and nail during the entire creative process. It is to his credit—and our benefit—that Titian followed his own directives until the end. Nevertheless, the friars were sufficiently displeased with the completed painting that they withheld payment to the artist for thirty years.

For logistical reasons, we'll interrupt our Titian theme here for just a moment and visit the sacristy altar, through the entryway on the right. First, though, note the only work in Venice by Donatello, the master sculptor from Florence: a wooden John the Baptist (1432), found just to the right of the main altar.

Inside the sacristy is a triptych commissioned by the Pesaro family and completed by Giovanni Bellini in 1488. This beautiful work in deep architectural relief presents Sts. Nicholas and Peter on the left, the Madonna and Child in the center, and Sts. Mark and Benedict on the right. The lovely frame—a work of art itself—was designed by Bellini and carved by Jacopo di Faenza.

Retracing our steps down the central aisle, we view the other masterpiece by Titian on the right: *The Ca' Pesaro Madonna*.

Also commissioned by the Pesaro family and unveiled on the Feast of the Immaculate Conception, December 8, in 1526, this painting marks a confident and radical departure from the (then) traditional conventions of visual narration. And together with *The Assumption*, it marks the beginning of an artistic era known as the High Renaissance: when sixteenth-century painters boldly created a "golden century" of Venetian art by playing up the sensual beauties of the real world and downplaying the less tangible attributes of the metaphysical world.

At first glance, *The Ca' Pesaro Madonna* shows Titian's more muted use of color. (Perhaps he'd learned from his previous experiences in trying to please the friars.) But this small compromise freed the artist to take an even greater chance: he positioned his primary subjects off center in an inverted-S composition and thus gave the work a greater sense of depth and reality. This successful experiment remains one of the most important contributions to the history of art.

In the foreground, among the adoring saints, are portraits of members of the Pesaro family. A young boy unabashedly locks eyes with the viewer, continually making an immediate connection between himself and every visitor who has seen him over these many centuries and who will see him in centuries to come.

It would be nice to report that Titian lived out his long, productive, and prosperous life as a compassionate, generous, and benign master artist, but that is not the case. In truth, he grew increasingly spiteful, penurious, and vindictive with every year's passing. Legend has it, for example, that after one day in his studio, Titian recognized the strong talent of Jacopo Tintoretto and out of jealousy banished the young man from his sight. In so doing, Titian created a nasty rivalry between the two, a game of artistic one-upmanship which many believe Tintoretto ultimately won. (Certainly this is true in the case of the Scuola di San Rocco, which we will visit next on this walk.)

Titian died on August 27, 1576, in a devastating plague that killed 51,000 people in eighteen months' time; he was eighty-six years old. Only days before, he'd watched his son die of the same disease. By then, perhaps, Titian's only comfort was knowing that he would be buried within this very church—but that almost didn't happen. Upon learning of the master's death, the panicked survivors threw Titian's body into a massive common grave and looted his home of all its possessions. It took the intervention of the doge himself to exhume the

Doors near the Scuola Grande di San Rocco

man's body and put it in its rightful resting place: a tomb just past the public entrance, on the left.

Built entirely of Carrara marble, this monument was sponsored through the generosity of Ferdinand I of Austria and completed in 1853 by two brothers, Luigi and Pietro Zandomeneghi. Beneath the winged lion of the Republic is a statue of Titian before a bas-relief representation of his *Assumption*. The heavy and ponderous neoclassical design is probably not at all what Titian would have envisioned for himself, but it stands here for all eternity as a loving tribute to the creative genius.

Directly behind us rises the pyramid monument to the sculptor Antonio Canova (1757–1822). Also of Carrara marble, the tomb was actually designed by Canova for Titian in 1794. The women represent Sculpture, Painting, and Architecture. The snake surrounding the artist's effigy symbolizes immortality. The lion, of course, represents Venice. This tomb, too, is neoclassic in style and seems sharply cold and out of place amid its surroundings. Inside, there is only the sculptor's heart.

Obviously, there is much, much more around us to see and discuss, but for now, only a few other highlights will have to suffice. Among the tombs of doges in the church, that to our immediate left, dating from 1659, is of Giovanni Pesaro. John Ruskin once erroneously described the full-scale statue of the doge as having "arms expanded, like an actor courting applause." Claudio Monteverdi is buried here as well, under the floor of the basilica. (In his honor, concerts are still given using the original organ.) The cloister here is lovely and worthy of another, longer visit. Before exiting, check out the sculptures over the doors; they're bound to make anyone reconsider his mortality.

Once out of the Frari, we head right and follow the white-on-maroon sign pointing to the Scuola Grande di San Rocco. As we pass the Frari's bell tower, let us note that it is about 230 feet, or 70 meters, high. The only one taller in Venice is the Campanile in Piazza San Marco.

The façade of the **Scuola Grande di San Rocco** (open 9:00–13:00 and 15:30–18:30) is best represented by Canaletto in *The Doge Visiting the Church and Scuola di San Rocco* on display in the Accademia. The painting depicts the custom of St. Roch's Day, August 16, when artists and dealers were allowed to come together in street-fair fashion and exhibit works for sale. The heritage of art patronage thus was nurtured inside as well as out.

According to John Ruskin, this building is one of the three most precious in the world; its collection of works by Jacopo Robusti, called Tintoretto (1518–1594), rank it right up there with the Sistine Chapel in Rome and the Camposanto in Pisa. The design and construction of the asymmetrical structure (1515–1560) are the work of Bartolomeo Bon and Antonio Abbondi, also called Scarpagnino. Its interior decorations celebrate Tintoretto's work—fifty-six paintings completed over twenty-four years' time—and place him at the forefront of Mannerist painters from the Venetian late Renaissance.

One can return here on many occasions and spend many hours happily lost amid thoughts and images. The relative quiet is a luxury. No matter the time of season, week, or day, the atmosphere inside this place seems truly rarefied: so few visitors, such vast galleries, and so many magnificent artworks. While on this walk, however, it is best to limit your visit to thirty minutes.

As the name implies, San Rocco is one of the six major *scuole* of Venice. In these halls met workers of the textile industry: importers, exporters, and merchants; weavers, printers, and dyers, *tintori*. As Tintoretto's nickname ("Little Dyer"), implies, his father, Battista Robusti, was a craftsman who belonged to a guild. Understandably, Tintoretto felt a deep affinity for this *scuola*. The work accomplished here was the most important to him personally, and he labored very hard to win the commission.

For this visit, we'll take a chronological approach, beginning upstairs in the smaller room in the back. To do this, walk up Abbondi's staircase, through the Sala Grande, and into the Sala dell'Albergo. So as not to spoil the effect later on, try not to pay too much attention to the works as you first pass through these great halls. Look at the beautiful inlay work in the floors instead.

When the Republic-wide competition was announced for the interior decoration of San Rocco in 1564, Tintoretto found himself vying against a number of heavyweight artists, Paolo Veronese, Francesco Salviati, and Federico Zuccari among them. To gain the advantage, while the other masters prepared their preliminary drawings, Tintoretto went ahead and at his own expense executed a full-scale painting, *The Glory of San Rocco*.

In the middle of the night before the presentations were to take place, he snuck into the Sala dell'Albergo, installed the work on the ceiling, and covered it with a curtain. The next morning, as other artists unrolled their sketches for consideration, Tintoretto stood in the corner empty-handed and quietly awaited his turn.

His moment arrived, and the curious judges watched as the brazen artist merely reached up, tugged once on a string dangling over his head, and sent the covering drapery fluttering down from the ceiling. There was only an instant of awestruck silence before competitors and sponsors alike erupted into angry protest. Tintoretto shrewdly offered the painting as a gift to the *scuola*, knowing full well that the order's charter forbade it from declining any charitable contribution.

Obviously, the ploy worked. Tintoretto was awarded the contract to provide three paintings a year, payment for which included a hundred ducats every twelve months plus a lifetime seat on the San Rocco's executive operating board. The artist's other works in this room include *Christ Before Pilate*, *Christ Bearing the Cross*, and an *Ecce Homo*.

Tintoretto's huge *Crucifixion*, which John Ruskin pronounced "beyond all analysis and above all praise," is a brilliant and arresting masterpiece of deliberately calculated scale. A provision in Tintoretto's contract stated that he leave one surface open for his archrival, Titian. The crafty artist refused to agree to the directive until after he had painted this largest wall, thus ensuring that any work by Titian would be of lesser importance. This most important treasure deserves our attention and appreciation.

The paintings decorating the ceiling and walls of the Sala Grande were executed between 1575 and 1581, with the exception of the altarpiece, *The Vision of San Rocco*, which was added in 1588. All of them were created to compensate for the hall's notable lack of natural illumination; each seems to glow with its own light from within. As we gaze around, every image reflects Tintoretto's superb draftsmanship and brilliant brushwork, which breaks up his color into functional and decorative patterns; the innovative technique is attributed directly to the artist.

The ceiling panels depict figures and episodes from the Old Testament, among them Adam and Eve, Jonah and the Whale, Jacob's Ladder, Moses Drawing Water from the Rock, the Brazen Serpent, and the Miracle of the Manna. The walls describe scenes from the New Testament: the Baptism, the Raising of Lazarus, the Feeding of the Five Thousand, and the Last Supper. In stylish continuity, the

Fall of Man overhead is connected iconographically to *The Nativity* and *The Temptation of Christ* below it.

In choosing these scenes, Tintoretto placed particular emphasis on representations of San Rocco's charitable work with those in need. It was believed at the time that all suffering was the direct result of punishment from God. Embodiments of Thirst, Disease, and Hunger hover above the room and plague the unholy beneath. While the ceiling threatens doom, the walls promise salvation through embracing the life of Christ.

Returning downstairs, we enter the ground-floor hall that Tintoretto devoted to decorations honoring the life of the Virgin Mary. Here we find depictions of the Adoration of the Magi, the Flight into Egypt, the Massacre of the Innocents, the Circumcision, and the Assumption. The first painting in the corner facing the entryway, *The Annunciation*, proves the most sensuous and daring.

Tintoretto died on May 31, 1594, and was buried in the Chiesa della Madonna dell'Orto (Walk 4), his parish church; it was his wish to lie beside his beloved daughter, Marietta, who had died four years before. His sons, Domenico and Marco, carried on the work in his studio, employing shadow-box models with miniature wax figurines and string grids to replicate their father's composition and perspective. Later, Tintoretto's son-in-law, Sebastiano Casser, inherited the operation and managed to keep it running until 1627.

For now, we bid farewell to Tintoretto and promise to return another day. We step outdoors, turn right, stroll back around the *campo*, and position ourselves so that the white-on-maroon sign is on our right.

Slip into the side street beside no. 3017. Follow the "Rialto" and "Vaporetto" signs straight ahead on Calle Larga. Notice how, in the building on the left, the first floor overhangs the street on corbels: a clever method of house expansion. Jag left/right on Ramo dei Caleghieri to Campo San Tomà. In the afternoon, it's common to find a street musician or two performing beside the well. From

111

here, you have a choice to make, depending on your reserves of interest and energy.

If you've had enough for now, head right and follow the "Vaporetto" signs to Calle dei Traghetto Vecchio and catch a waterbus back to Piazza San Marco.

If you're up for a little more exploration, turn left toward Rialto San Marco or Traghetto San Tomà. Cross Campiello San Tomà diagonally and then cross over Ponte San Tomà to see **Casa Goldoni,** the home of Carlo Goldoni (1707–1793), on the right across the canal; beyond its inner well-head and staircase, the building houses a museum and a library honoring the great Venetian playwright (open 8:30–13:30).

Now you're on Calle dei Nomboli. Turn left onto Rio Terà dei Nomboli. The next right puts you on the narrow Calle dei Saoneri, where, at no. 2747, you will find the shop of a most unusual and exquisite glassworks artisan: **Amadi**. In delicate and intricate life-size detail, with an entomologist's knowledge and precision, he creates all sorts of insects in glass. A number of Murano-trained glassblowers sell similar products around town, but this artist's creations are of matchless refinement, especially his winged creatures. Even a brief stop inside will tempt you to pick up a number of these fascinating bugs; they make terrific gifts.

Cross Ponte San Polo, proceed along Salizada San Polo, go straight past Campo San Polo, and take Calle de la Madoneta. Proceed over Ponte de la Madoneta, pass under the archway, and intersect Calle del Forno. Look left to Ramo del Magazen no. 1469. There, you will meet one of sculptor **Matteo Lo Grecco**'s famous, frivolous, fanciful fat women, poised lightly on tiptoe on a pedestal. Check out his studio, sign his guest book, and meet a few more of his larger-than-life Madonnas.

Heading home now, walk through Campiello dei Meloni, bear right, and follow signs saying "Per Rialto e San Marco" on Calle de Mezo. Cross Campo San Aponal; follow the "Rialto" sign to Calle del Luganegher. After cross-

Outside the studio of Matteo Lo Grecco

ing Campo San Silvestro diagonally and passing under Sottoportego del Tragheto, you will reach the Canal Grande within eyesight of Ponte Rialto. From here, you can take a *vaporetto* to any point in the city or cross the bridge for a quick stroll back to Piazza San Marco.

One more suggestion? Take the *traghetto* across the Canal. Even though you'll probably have to ride the boat standing up, it's the most inexpensive way any visitor can ride in an authentic gondola. (Watch your balance!)

Walk · 3

Courtesans,
Gondoliers, and Peggy

TO THE ACCADEMIA
AND ALONG THE ZATTERE

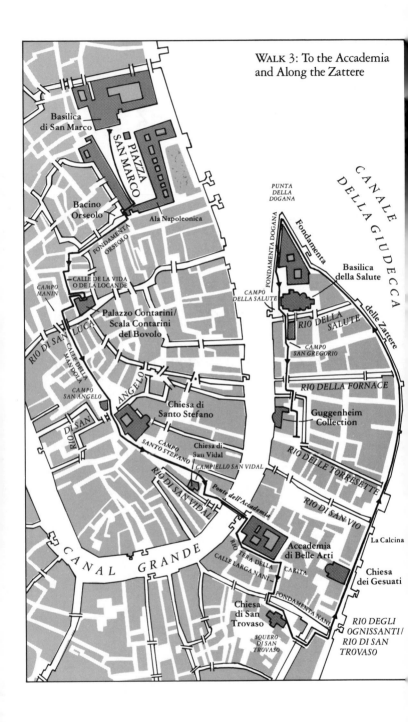

WALK 3: To the Accademia
and Along the Zattere

Basilica
di San Marco

PIAZZA
SAN MARCO

CANALE
DELLA GIUDECCA

PUNTA
DELLA
DOGANA

Bacino
Orseolo

FONDAMENTA DOGANA

Fondamenta

Ala Napoleonica

FONDAMENTA
ORSEOLO

Basilica
della Salute

CALLE DE LA VIDA
O DE LA LOCANDE

CAMPO
MANIN

CAMPO
DELLA SALUTE

delle Zattere

CALLE DELLA MANDOLA

Palazzo Contarini/
Scala Contarini
del Bovolo

RIO DELLA
SALUTE

RIO DI SAN LUCA

CAMPO
SAN GREGORIO

ANGELO

CAMPO
SAN ANGELO

RIO DELLA FORNACE

Chiesa di
Santo Stefano

Guggenheim
Collection

DI SAN

Chiesa di
San Vidal

CAMPO
SANTO STEFANO

CAMPIELLO SAN VIDAL

RIO DELLE TORRESETTE

RIO DI SAN VIDAL

Ponte dell'Accademia

RIO DI SAN VIO

CANAL
GRANDE

RIO TERA DELLA CARITA

Accademia
di Belle Arti

La Calcina

CALLE LARGA NANI

Chiesa
dei Gesuati

Chiesa di
San Trovaso

FONDAMENTA NANI

RIO DEGLI
OGNISSANTI/
RIO DI SAN
TROVASO

SQUERO
DI SAN
TROVASO

Starting Point: Piazza San Marco

This walk is long in distance, time, and text. And with it, one must choose either of two schedules: between 9:00 and 13:30 or 14:30 and 18:30. A morning itinerary will allow an abbreviated tour of the Basilica, which opens at 9:30, and a chance to visit the Guggenheim Collection, which opens at 12:30. An afternoon itinerary will allow for a longer visit inside the Basilica but will exclude a tour of the Accademia, which is closed later in the day.

Once again, we stand in the middle of Piazza San Marco with the **Basilica di San Marco** looming before us. By late afternoon, when the sun hangs wide in the west, the Basilica's gilded mosaic façade will shine with a light all its own and create a brilliant backdrop to this vast and wondrous space.

The Piazza was—and still is—the showcase of Venice, designed specifically as a stage for receptions to welcome visiting dignitaries, for religious processions, and for the annual presentation of the doge to his people. Huge, lavish affairs they were, involving hundreds of participants and thousands of spectators.

Practically every Venetian painter of merit has recorded the spectacles that took place in the Piazza. Every one of these events was intended to glorify the Republic, not the individuals taking part. And every structure you see here—including the Basilica—was originally built for political purposes.

The first building on this site was constructed as a chapel for Doge Giustiniano Partecipazio in 829 and consecrated in 832. It was created to entomb the body of the evangelist Mark, which had been delivered to Venice in 828 by two enterprising fishermen. (To recap briefly from the introductory "History" section: The fishermen broke into St. Mark's tomb in Alexandria, where he had been martyred; slipped the body of St. Claudia in place of the evangelist's; packed the—alas, headless—body into a large basket and disguised the true contents by covering the relic with pork. The Islamic guards were so repulsed by the meat that they waved the basket through without even touching it.)

To legitimize the theft, Venice quickly fabricated a prophecy claiming that St. Mark had actually visited the Lagoon during his lifetime. Supposedly blown in from the sea, he fell asleep on the Rialto and was visited by angels who said, *"Pax tibi, Marce evangelista. Hic requiescet corpus tuum"* ("Peace be unto thee, evangelist Mark. Here your body will rest").

During an uprising in 976, the original chapel was destroyed in a fire. The bones of St. Mark disappeared in the catastrophe but were recovered around 1094 after an early version of the present Basilica was completed under Doge Domenico Contarini.

Constructed of bricks atop pylons, this Basilica is a hodgepodge of late Roman, Byzantine, Gothic, and Renaissance styles. Built on the plan of the Greek cross, it was to rival the Basilica of the Twelve Apostles in Constantinople. Funding for the work was provided completely by the Venetian government, which thereby created a state church much like Westminster Abbey in London. Since 1807, St. Mark's has been the see of the patriarch of Venice.

Approaching the fantasy-like Basilica, we stop among the three cast-bronze flagstaffs, beautiful works by the sculptor and goldsmith Alessandro Leopardi completed in 1505. (Every Sunday morning at nine, and on political occasions as well, a small platoon of soldiers parades through the Piazza and raises a flag of Italy between two billowing gonfalons adorned with the winged lion of the Republic. At 18:30, a similar ceremony lowers them.) From this vantage point, we peer over the heads of tourists and take in the façade in all its intricate, luminescent detail.

St. Mark's façade is the largest of its style in the world. Inside and out, the mosaics cover a total area of 45,622 square feet, or 4,240 square meters. Creating the marble, gold, and colored-glass mosaics was an ongoing, Republic-wide process that took more than eight hundred years to complete. Naturally, styles and techniques—even available materials—changed over that time, and architectural differentiations are evident throughout the final work.

Greek and Byzantine artisans began the process in the eleventh century, concentrating on geometric and floral designs. In the twelfth century, local masters took up the task, incorporating human and animal forms into the mosaic work. But by the fifteenth century, native craftsmen had pretty much died out, so Paolo Uccello was brought in from Tuscany in 1424 to take over the workshop and introduce Florentine techniques; these are best seen on the interior walls and ceiling.

Outside, only the first lunette on the left contains original thirteenth-century mosaics. The scene depicts the transferral of the body of St. Mark into the Basilica as it once existed. Over the second door, we see the adoration of the body, done by Sebastiano Ricci in 1718. The central portal is decorated with a *Last Judgment* from the nineteenth century. The fourth lunette shows Venice welcoming the body of St. Mark. And the fifth describes the removal of the body from Alexandria.

Above these five lunettes are four scenes representing the death, resurrection, and ascension of Christ. Reproductions of the Four Horses adorn the gallery in the middle. The originals are inside, away from harmful pollution. (We will visit them shortly.) And above all this stands St. Mark, atop an angelic staircase, as if blessing all of Venice with his grace.

When you step through the central portal and enter the atrium, note first the diamond-shaped stone set in the floor. It marks the spot where two warring leaders, Pope Alexander III and Holy Roman Emperor Frederick I (who had recently been defeated by the Lombard League), met and made possible the Peace of Venice in 1177.

On the ceiling are scenes devoted to stories from the Old Testament. The legends of the Creation (which is extraordinarily depicted), Adam and Eve, Cain and Abel, Noah, the Tower of Babel, Abraham, Jacob, Joseph, and Moses are all spelled out in mosaic tiles as small as the faces of dice. Inside, we will see incidents from the life of Christ and episodes from the New Testament, grouped with scenes from the life of the Virgin Mary.

Be prepared to be overwhelmed by the opulence and splendor of everything around you when you enter the Basilica. This is one of the most grandiose environments on earth. It was a bold objective, indeed, for any government to erect such an edifice to its own honor. St. Mark's Basilica is one of the only interiors intended to glorify God *and* Man equally.

As we make our way behind the main altar (beneath which the body of St. Mark is buried), we should remark that the elaborate state ceremonies that once took place here fostered a rich musical heritage in Venice. The Republic became even more famous for this than for the visual arts. Great musicians served as masters of music for St. Mark's, among them Andrea Gabrieli, Claudio Monteverdi, Benedetto Marcello, Tommaso Albinoni, and Giovanni Battista Vivaldi, Antonio's father.

And it was here, in the late sixteenth century, that Giovanni Gabrieli, Andrea's nephew, extrapolated and elaborated existing themes and conventions to create polyphonic music. His compositions and arrangements for two organs, dissonantly playing opposite each other, and forty musicians divided into two choir groups revolutionized the music of the era. Without calling it so, he invented the stereophonic music we know so well today.

Reaching the far back of the Basilica, we discover the breathtaking **Pala d'Oro**, a golden altar screen, one of the true treasures of San Marco. Its first manifestation was commissioned in Constantinople around 976 by Doge Pietro Orseolo I (whom we will meet again soon). It was further refined, remodeled, and enlarged in 1105 by order of Doge Ordelafo Falier. In 1209, Doge Pietro Ziani had it adorned with additional gold, pearls, precious stones, and Byzantine enamels from the Monastery of Pantocrator. (All of the precious materials are loot from the Venetian sacking of Constantinople in 1204.) The screen was rearranged, completed in its present form, and signed by the goldsmith Gianpaolo Boninsegna, who installed it in its Gothic frame in 1345.

Among the eighty enamels adorning the Pala d'Oro are representations of Christ, the Virgin Mary, St. Mark, St. Michael, angels, prophets, evangelists, and the emperors of the East. It is encrusted with 1,300 pearls, 400 garnets, 300 sapphires, 90 amethysts, 90 rubies, 4 topazes, and 2 cameos. No one has ever attempted to establish its worth; everyone knows it is invaluable.

As you begin to exit the Basilica, note the dark stone statues across the top of the rood screen, which is the crucifix-adorned iconostasis dividing the chapel and the main altar. The sculptures were fashioned from *bronzetto* marble, so called for its color, about a hundred years before the time of Michelangelo and represent Mary, the apostles, and St. Mark on the left.

As we step back through the central doors of the Basilica, we see the stairway leading up to the **Museo Marciano**, where the Four Horses are displayed. Upon reaching the upper level, we are afforded a wonderful view of the Basilica's interior and a closer look at the ceiling mosaics. Outside, another vista widens before us, that of the entire Piazza; this is a perfect place from which

The original Four Horses

to take photographs. The horses we see here are fine reproductions of the ones we will visit next.

Reenter the interior and move to the left; you will discover the little chamber where the original **Four Horses** await. No one knows for sure, but most believe that these magnificent fourth-century Greco-Roman sculptures originated in Rome and were brought to the Hippodrome, the great racetrack of Constantinople, by Emperor Constantine himself. Carted off to Venice as spoils of war after Constantinople fell in 1204, the statues were placed first at the Arsenale and moved later to the Basilica. Also known as the "Bronze Horses of San Marco," they are in fact cast of an alloy consisting of ninety-eight percent copper and the rest gold and silver.

Venice traditionally displays these creatures as we see them here, in intimate pairs, but this is not the classical configuration, which would have the outer two horses turning outward and the middle two drawn together. If we consider that the artist most certainly designed them with a single light source in mind, however, a study of the *punti luminosi*, the crescents in their eyes, tells us that a third configuration was probably intended; two horses turning to the left and two to the right.

The numerous scratches and scorings across the horses' bodies were once thought to be the result of vandalism, but closer study has revealed that these marks were made intentionally with a single sharp instrument shortly after the horses received their gilding. Possibly the sun's reflection off their smooth gold surfaces frightened real horses and blinded chariot drivers on the Hippodrome track below. Some poor slave was then sent clambering up to the top of the Hippodrome to "take down the shine a bit" on the horses.

It has been said that every time these horses have moved, an empire has fallen, and that certainly appears to be true. When Rome fell they made their home in Byzantium. With Constantinople's collapse, they arrived in Venice. Napoleon transported them to Paris in 1807, after he had conquered the Republic; they were returned after Bonaparte's defeat at Waterloo. During World War I they were shipped off to Rome for safekeeping, and again during World War II they were removed from their position of honor. As the world becomes a more peaceful place in which to live, let's hope that these beautiful creatures are finally home to stay.

We exit the Basilica and walk toward the Ala Napoleonica to the far right corner of the Piazza. Directly ahead is **Giordan,** a fine jewelry store where you might shop for cameos and objects in gold and precious stones (tel. 5224289). It is also one of the exclusive shops where you can find antique and modern works in tortoiseshell. The little store is owned by a pleasant and demonstrative man named Giorgio, who is an avid fan of Milan's soccer teams and who can often be spotted in the *campi* or on the Lido playing a favorite Venetian card game—*scopa*—with his many friends.

Out the last exit on the right, we walk under Sottoportego de l'Arco Celeste to find the **Bacino Orseolo,** a boat basin formed in 1869 by widening a dead-end canal

Keystone lion in Piazza San Marco

so that gondoliers could park their boats by night and reach closer to Piazza San Marco to find their customers by day.

With the Hotel Cavalletto & Doge Orseolo in the background, two dozen or more gondolas are usually found nestled together in this watery expanse. Here the boatmen gather each morning to catch up on news and receive their daily assignments and schedules from a clipboard-wielding dispatcher who works much like one at an airport taxi stand. Throughout Venice, there are fewer than a dozen prime locations out of which gondoliers work, and with some four hundred commercial licenses currently on issue, the gondoliers are rotated within their stations every day to give each one an equal opportunity for business.

As passengers await their turn, each boatman swings out from the raft of gondolas, nudges his boat through the congestion with his oar, and comes broadside against the wide stone steps. Graciously, he helps his clients aboard before inserting his *forcola*, oarlock, into its slot and rowing away down the canal. You may wish to rest against a railing here and read a bit ahead before proceeding along this walk.

The basin is named for the Orseolo family, which produced three doges. Pietro I was the first. He began the rebuilding of St. Mark's Basilica after the fire of 976. He also founded a number of hospices and almshouses throughout the city. One, the Orsoline, stood where the Hotel Cavalletto stands now. After only two years in office, Orseolo underwent a religious crisis of some sort and retired to a monastery. He was canonized after his death.

The second doge in the family was Pietro I's son, Pietro II, who was installed into office in 991. He was the right man for the job. Under his rule, quarreling factions within Venice were calmed and united with a new sense of purpose. New trading agreements were negotiated with Constantinople, and—Pietro II knew how to play both ends expertly off the middle—warm diplomatic relationships were nurtured with the Holy Roman Emperor, Otto III.

Nine years into his reign—on May 9, 1000, after Ascension Day mass—Pietro II boarded a warship and led his fleet on a most important and long-overdue mission.

The two previous centuries had brought upon Venetian vessels a plague of pirates from Croatia, across the Adriatic. Their murderous raids on tradesmen's ships had continually weakened and compromised Venetian operations, and the time was right to put an end to their actions once and for all.

Down the coast of Dalmatia the doge sailed, defeating and subjugating all in his way. Upon his return, not only had Pietro II ensured a safe route across the sea, he had laid the foundation of Venice's maritime power. And by controlling vast tracks of (foreign—what is now Yugoslavian) timberland and farmland, he more than satisfied the Republic's appetites for food and raw materials.

Pietro II, too, seems to have undergone a deep personal crisis. In 1006, he suddenly installed his sixteen-year-old son, Otto, on the ducal throne, bequeathed his estate to the Church and the poor, abandoned his wife and family, and retired to a far wing in the palace. He died quietly less than two years later.

Otto Orseolo, the youngest doge in Venetian history, apparently proved himself to be quite capable. "Catholic in faith, calm in purity, strong in justice, eminent in religion, decorous in his manner of life, well endowed with wealth and possessions, and so filled with all forms of virtue that he was universally considered to be the most fitting successor of his father and grandfather," Andrea Dandalo (who was the fourth and last doge in his family, from 1343 to 1354) wrote of Otto three centuries later.

Such was one review of Otto's early performance. We suspect, however, that the author was a bit too inclined to wax nearly poetic on the idea of family rule. Old Otto just wasn't that good a guy. His subjects knew him as an ambitious and power-hungry young man.

Ten years into his reign, Doge Otto, who was then only twenty-seven, appointed his brother Orso, who was thirty, to be patriarch of Grado. Otto's other brother, twenty-year-old Vitale, was made bishop of Torcello. A mistake if there ever was one. Suddenly, these three "kids" had all of Venice as their playground. And their classic sibling rivalries and petty jealousies created a hornet's nest of greed and opportunism throughout the Republic. Finally, in 1026, Venetians put an end to the chaos by forcibly seizing Otto, shaving his beard, removing him from office, and exiling him to Constantinople.

The Hotel Cavalletto across the basin was built in the

fourteenth century and named for the horses, *cavalli*, that once were a principal mode of transportation in Venice and were stabled nearby. (Imagine how crowded these narrow streets must have been back when there were people *and horses* to contend with!)

Walk along the *fondamenta* to your left; perhaps you'll follow a gondola full of tourists beginning their adventure and happily snapping pictures.

Just ahead, Ponte Tron o de la Piavola forms a graceful arch over the canal. Many will want to continue straight ahead, but for those looking for an unusual shopping experience, a slight detour is recommended. Turn left opposite the bridge onto Calle Tron. At its end, straight ahead, the narrow Frezzaria forms a T intersection with it. Turn right, then left, walk past shops selling shoes and lingerie, and notice one, at no. 1770, offering exquisitely ornate masks, enchanting marionettes, antique canes, Carnival costumes, and traditional Murano glassware.

This is **Il Prato** (tel. 5203375). Janna (pronounced "Yahna") is the name of the lovely Yugoslavian woman who works inside. The masks for sale here are ornamental in nature and not to be worn. They're expensive, expansive, diaphanous creations of gilded metal screening, lace, and crystal beads and are best displayed on a wall, safely away from the crush of the Carnival crowd.

Back to Ponte Tron o de la Piavola, continue away from the Bacino Orseolo along the *fondamenta* and across Ponte Goldoni. Where the Banca Nazionale del Lavoro is now, there was once the House of the Francesconi. It is here that the illustrious neoclassic sculptor Antonio Canova died on October 13, 1822, at age sixty-four.

Bear left past Campiello de la Regina d'Ungheria and go under Sottoportego de la Malvasia. Following the yellow signs to "Scala Contarini del Bovolo," turn right, take the first left, and follow Calle de la Vida o de le Locande. Turn left again under the arch and enter Calle e Corte Contarini del Bovolo.

Here, on the right behind a black iron fence, amid

a little courtyard littered with antique sculptural fragments and a dozen or more cats, you will find **Palazzo Contarini** with its unique exterior spiral staircase, the **Scala del Bovolo** (*bovolo* means "snail's shell" in Venetian). This fanciful Renaissance stairway was designed by a protégé of Mauro Coducci, Giovanni Canali, around 1499. How perfect a setting for a Shakespearean play! It's easy to imagine Othello, the Moor of Venice, ascending these stairs and delivering a climactic soliloquy. In 1771, fifteen-year-old Mozart lived as a neighbor across the way.

Backtrack a bit and turn left on the narrow Calle de la Vida o de le Locande. Follow the street to the right and enter the center of **Campo Manin.** Here stands a statue honoring the Venetian hero Daniele Manin (whom we met at the start of Walk 1), before the headquarters of the principal bank of Venice, the Cassa di Risparmio di Venezia. Known by its neighbors as the "Ugly Bank," it is the most prominent and recent intrusion into the *centro storico*, or historical center. The architect Pier Luigi Nervi is responsible for this unfortunate structure, which he completed in 1964 using themes from his building designs for the Rome Summer Olympics in 1960. Most folks wish those themes had stayed back in Rome, where they belong.

Cross the first bridge on the left, the Ponte de la Cortesia (named for the courtesans who lived in this area; we'll meet them soon). Follow signs reading "Accademia" along Calle de la Cortesia (also known as Calle de la Mandola) and into **Campo San Angelo.** This wide-open space is distinguished primarily by its view of the disconcertingly tilted bell tower of the Chiesa di Santo Stefano beyond it, and then by four fifteenth-century Gothic structures surrounding it (among them, Palazzo Duodo and Palazzo Gritti). Note the characteristic three-lobed Gothic arches in the windows of the buildings to the right and left. The Venetian composer Domenico Cimarosa lived and died at no. 3584.

Wellhead

In this *campo* you will find real Venetians living their daily lives. Businesspeople congregate around the newsstands and keep tabs on the world headlines, market values, and sports scores; children scamper more after each other than after their ubiquitous soccer balls; and the older folks sit back calmly, taking it all in and basking in the sun.

So large is this space that during summer film festivals hundreds gather at night to watch the latest movies projected on a large outdoor screen. In decades past, the circus performed here whenever it came to town.

Cross the *campo* toward your right and peek inside the doors of the Intendenza di Finanza, the tax office, just to the left of Ponte dei Frati. There you will see the original Chiostro di Santo Stefano, attributed to the sixteenth-century designer Antonio Abbondi. On his way to Rome around 1510, Martin Luther passed through Venice and lodged at this cloister. He also celebrated mass at Santo Stefano's high altar.

Just ahead, beside the porcelain shop at no. 3535, a scruffy little black dog, whom we've nicknamed "Sneakers," can usually be found asleep at the curb, unruffled by the constant parade of alien feet. Tiptoe by and let him nap.

Ahead on our left we come to the beautiful **Chiesa di Santo Stefano** (open 9:00–12:00 and 16:00–18:00), which was completed in 1374 by Augustinian monks who were famous for the plays they produced. The foliage-adorned Gothic portal was added by Bartolomeo Bon in the fifteenth century. As we step inside, keep in mind that this church is actually built on two islands. It may be the only church in the world with a canal flowing under its main altar.

The interior is a rare gem of Venetian architecture; the ceiling is unusual, its wooden sprung beams suggesting the shipbuilding techniques of the Arsenale. In fact, this is known as a ship's-keel ceiling, and only one other church in Venice—San Giacomo dell'Orio—has a similar ceiling. The superb woodwork enhances—and is enhanced by—the light, airy, and peaceful atmosphere of the interior. (Apparently that wasn't always the case. It has been claimed that this church was rebuilt six times, because as many assassinations took place inside.)

Paintings here include Nicolò Bambini's *Birth of the Virgin*, over the first altar on the right, and Tintoretto's works in the sacristy: *Christ Washing the Feet of the Apostles, The Prayer on the Mount of Olives,* and *The Last Supper,* the last actually executed by a member of Tintoretto's school and not the master himself. Gaspare Diziani's brightly colored *Massacre of the Innocents* (1733) over the door is probably this minor painter's one and only masterpiece. Works by Jacopo Palma the Elder (Palma Vecchio), Bartolomeo Vivarini, and Paris Bordone can be seen as well here.

The church is famous more for its sculpture than its painting. Around the chancel stand rather stiff statues from the Lombardo school; at one time they decorated an altar screen. Much finer are the three statues, attributed directly to Pietro Lombardo and his sons, on the third altar on the left, and the entrance-wall monument to Giacomo Surian with its effigy reliefs.

Next to the Surian monument is Antonio Canova's monument to his first patron, Giovanni Falier. Canova did some of his first carvings in the church's cloister, where he had his studio.

The high altar is a beautiful work dated 1661. The intricately carved monks' choir behind the altar was done by Marco and Francesco Cozzi (who also carved the Frari stalls and a ceiling in the Accademia) in 1488. To the right of the sacristy door is a bronze relief, *The Virgin and Child with Saints and Donors*, by Alessandro Leopardi, who cast Verrocchio's Colleoni statue (Walk 4).

Giovanni Gabrieli, one of the best composers of his era and organist of San Marco from 1585 to 1612, is buried under the slab before the first altar on the left.

Exiting the church and turning to our left, we see a fine restaurant, **Memi,** across the street; it serves hearty traditional Venetian fish, *risotto,* and pasta dishes. If you return here around eight-thirty at night, you'll find the local hangout filled with native craftsmen, artists, writers, actors, and intellectuals. It's a good place for a casual supper, especially in the summer months when tables are set up outside on the deck. The sixteenth-century building in which it is housed was once a *scuola,* which Vittore Carpaccio decorated; the paintings now hang in the Brera in Milan and the Ca' d'Oro in Venice (Walk 4).

Toward the end of Calle Longa on the right is another good restaurant, **Al Baccaretto**, where the locals go for lunch. In the evening, the atmosphere becomes more buoyant when neighborhood families come to dine. Fish soup, bean soup, *pasticcio di pesce* (lasagne with fish), *bacalà* (cod stew), and *fegato alla veneziana* (Venetian-style liver) are recommended here.

A few steps away is **Campo Santo Stefano** (in some guidebooks called "Campo Francesco Morosini," after the man who blew the lid off the Parthenon in Athens in 1687; his home is to the distant left of the *campo*). On your immediate right, the bar **Paolin** serves some of the best *gelato* in all of Venice. The flavors are distinct and delicious; *nocciola*, hazelnut, is a real favorite.

Campo Santo Stefano is an airy, sunlit space where businesspeople shuttle by, children frolic, and tourists sit at outdoor tables and enjoy the scenery. Five hundred years ago, visitors here enjoyed another type of "scenery" that made Venice one of the most popular vacation destinations in the world: courtesans. Perhaps we should stop at a green umbrella-table, have some refreshment, and imagine their provocative lives.

Beginning with the earliest Crusades in the twelfth century, Venice learned the real value of hospitality. As shipping agents for the Holy Wars, Venice received tens of thousands of hardy recruits every week. They streamed into the city from all over Europe, ready, willing, and able to be assigned to well-equipped galleys and shipped off to war.

Naturally, the outflow of troops could not keep up with the daily infusion of mercenaries and volunteers. And it didn't take Venetian businessmen long to realize that the expected delays and layovers these restless men experienced meant sizable profits for Venetian churches, shops, eateries, casinos, taverns, and inns.

Entertainment became a major industry in Venice, and prostitution flourished over the next three hundred years. A specialized and sophisticated sort of "kept woman" evolved and took her place amid Venetian high society. These women did so well that by the fifteenth century, some 14,000 legally registered taxpaying courtesans lived in the city, many of them around this very *campo*. (This does not include an even greater number of pimps, street prostitutes, transvestites, nuns, and wayward wives who also derived income from such pastimes.)

Venetian wives of this era were kept isolated inside the home by their husbands, jealously guarded from wanton strangers and licentious neighbors. A niche existed within Venetian society that was masterfully filled by this special breed of public woman. Accessible to men day and night, the courtesans were encouraged by the government to spy on clients from out of town and were widely considered the only real preventive "cure" for homosexuality. Placing himself in so vulnerable a position between mistress and wife, the Venetian male idealized the courtesan as the consummate keeper of secrets and teller of truths: a heady position, indeed, with a heavy responsibility to bear.

Courtesans were revered in literature as "honest" and "sumptuous," "tantalizing and pure." Their faces and bodies inspired countless portraits by the greatest artists of their time. Their clothing and hairstyles inspired new fashions around the world. These high-rent women constituted a considerable and respectable stratum of Venetian society, an elite class of educated, wealthy, liberated, and self-sufficient women who answered to no man and were in complete control of their lives.

This was a rarity among women anywhere in the world. (Indeed, unfortunately that's true even today.) And while Venice was one of the first governments to foster women's rights—allowing them to inherit assets directly or file lawsuits on their own behalf, for instance—career outlets for single women past "marriageable age" were few and far between. Basically, a woman had two choices: enter a convent or become a prostitute. (And as we learned in Walk 1 with the nuns of San Zaccaria, sometimes there was little difference between the two occupations!)

These "professional ladies" took very seriously their

position in life. Many became accomplished students of foreign languages, literature, music, science, and business. And they used their learning to charm and captivate their clients and enhance their reputations.

Often, a courtesan of good repute maintained a steady clientele of five or six regular patrons, who paid handsomely for their one-night-a-week visits. (The women firmly maintained their freedom by day and reserved the right to entertain foreigners in the off-hours, frequently amid gatherings of artists and scholars, high-ranking priests, and wealthy tradesmen.)

A courtesan's day was, quite literally, luxurious. Such a woman awakened in late morning and was served breakfast in bed, then idled in her bath until just before midday. Maybe she received tutoring in Latin or Greek while she rinsed her hair with fragrant concoctions of boiled vine ash, barley shafts, twig bark, licorice, and lime juice. Or maybe she discussed real estate with her accountant while she received her massage.

As the sun reached its zenith, she and her companions made their way to a rooftop loggia, the *altana*, where she wore shimmering silks and donned a broad-brimmed straw hat, a *solana*, to shade her pearly complexion. The hat had a large hole in the top, through which she pulled her tresses to dry and bleach them in the sun. Maybe she wrote poetry to a lover—or notes of intrigue to an official in the government—while she gossiped about one client's endowments and another's deficiency. Maybe she practiced the lute, knowing full well that a number of young gentlemen always gathered on the street below whenever she played. (She'd have her pick of them yet!)

Vittore Carpaccio's *Two Courtesans*, which hangs in the Museo Correr, presents the young women as fair . . . and fairly bored. Decked out in all their finery, they sit passively on their terrace amid a menagerie of dwarves, dogs, and exotic birds. On the left, a pair of absurdly high platform shoes, *pianelle*, can be found. These were all the rage among the elite. The wobbly things—often a foot high or more—held skirt hems above the soiling streets and added stature to their mystique.

By afternoon, a courtesan moved downstairs to her boudoir, where she nibbled on whatnots and beautified herself in the Murano-glass mirrors of her toilet. Maybe she gave last-minute orders to her kitchen staff while she applied a new blush to her cheeks. Maybe she modeled different outfits for the eager members of her salon in the music room. Or received into her inner chambers a gentleman caller from faraway Arabia. Or stretched out and posed naked for a master artist who transformed her into a Greek goddess across his canvas.

Soon it was time for a *passeggiata*, a stroll around the *campo* to display her wares in public. Usually accompanied by two handmaidens—one holding the train of her dress, the other steadying her shaky gait—she floated out among the people and flirted her way through society. Maybe she coyly bared her breasts to one prospective client or lifted her skirts to reveal man's trousers to another who might be interested in something else. Every move was choreographed.

The full-blown productions were reserved for nighttime feasts. Here the hostess pulled out all the stops and bathed her "special sponsors" in sumptuous, sensuous splendor.

Angela del Moro (a.k.a. "La Zaffetta," because her father was a policemen, a *zaffo*) was one such courtesan; she often entertained her men in the lights of Venetian superstardom. The likes of Jacopo Sansovino, Titian, and Pietro Aretino stimulated conversations around her table bedecked with roast pheasant and peacock, seasoned game and fish. (One such banquet involved twenty-two courses, one of which was a whole roasted, gold-leafed ostrich!)

The poet Niccolò Franco credited La Zaffetta with reintroducing culinary splendor into Venetian society in his *Epistle to Whores*: "Not only have you revived a lost age, but you have brought it back in grand style, eliminating everything rustic and coarse. Instead of acorns, blackberries, and strawberries, you propose sumptuous platters and set elaborate tables covered with richly woven cloths appropriate for such delicate foods."

But Lynne Lawner, in her *Lives of the Courtesans*, tells us that Angela del Moro was made to suffer greatly at the hands of one jealous patron and seventy-nine despicable cohorts. Sometimes a courtesan would fall out of favor with a client. Usually this meant that angry letters were exchanged, certain gifts were returned, any future financial support was cut off, and that was that. But one Lorenzo Venier, supposed client of La Zaffetta's, relied on an ancient form of revenge against courtesans known as a *trentuno*, literally "thirty-one," which he later described in a nine-hundred-line satirical poem entitled *Il Trentuno della Zaffetta*.

Basically, a "thirty-one" was premeditated gang rape, designed to sully the woman's reputation, possibly expose her to venereal disease, and destroy her livelihood. And for very unfortunate victims, a "royal thirty-one" involved eighty men. On April 6, 1531, on the island of Chioggia, La Zaffetta was given the "royal treatment."

It is a tribute to her fortitude that Angela survived her ordeal. More impressive still was the fact that she managed to maintain a lofty position within that exotic society and continued to court notoriety. In later life, she became one of the sponsors of bull-baiting spectacles, which were staged right here in Campo Santo Stefano (as depicted in the 1628 painting *Courtesans Bull-baiting* by Giacomo Franco, exhibited in the Museo Correr).

This courtesan sponsorship of sports spectaculars to arouse the interest of male clients became common practice. And as late as the eighteenth century, these sporty women raced their private gondolas every year in the northern sector of the city above the Ghetto. Gabriel Bella captured the event in a (rather crude) painting entitled *Courtesans Racing in the Rio della Sensa*, which hangs in the Palazzo Querini-Stampalia (Walk 4).

On Carnival nights of yesteryear, the temptresses swooped through this *campo* as if from myth. With their images further enhanced by costumes and masks, they enticed and enchanted their men with mystery, secrecy, and daring. How many men fell under their spell? How many more would do so even today?

If at this moment you are, indeed, seated at a green umbrella-table, you are most likely patronizing one of the busiest and most popular pizzerias in the city. Although it displays no name to the public, the two gentlemen who own it, Lino and Guido, affectionately call their establishment **De Vidi**, after the elderly woman who ran it before them. The restaurant's prime location (no. 9797–9898, at a major crossroads between Piazza San Marco and the Rialto and Accademia Bridges) contributes to its popularity, but its fare, designed to cater to tourists—Americans in particular—makes it special.

Here is where you can find large salads and fruit dishes and even larger steins of draft beer. The house white wine is among the best in the city. Few are the passersby who can resist temptation upon seeing the fresh-picked fruit and vegetables in outside display coolers. Fewer still are the patrons who can sit beside another enjoying a large bowl of seasonal berries and ice cream and not say, "I want one of *those*!"

The waiters here are especially congenial. And do not misunderstand their inclination to leave you alone for long periods of time—you'll have to flag one down to ask for the *conto*, or check—it's just that they believe their customers deserve leisurely privacy. Venice is one place where a customer can dawdle and daydream all morning over a single cup of coffee and not feel guilty about taking up a table. You may find yourself returning here in the evening and staying until closing time, around one in the morning.

In the center of the *campo*—a favorite gathering place of neighborhood children and parents—a statue of Niccolò Tommaseo by Francesco Barzaghi peers down on the oasis of shade under green canvas. No doubt pigeons perch all over him as you read this. (The statute of Old Niccolò is called "The Book S—itter" by natives, because it makes it appear as if the statesman's literary works were produced by defecation rather than inspiration.)

Continuing across the *campo*, we see the Chiesa di San Vidal (Vitale) ahead on our right. Today it's an art gallery; Carpaccio's original painting of the saint on horseback can still be seen inside. Closer on the left, an imaginative clothes shop sports intricately beaded outfits on woodenly bearded mannequins. (At least go peek in the window; they're really quite an eyeful.) Just ahead, the *campo* opens more to the left. If you listen closely, you might hear an aria or a cello solo from Palazzo Pizanni beyond; it is a music conservatory now.

The flower shop tucked into the corner of Campiello San Vidal is lush, shaded by dripping foliage from the beautiful, private Ca' Franchetti gardens behind it. One might think the blossoms in the shop were grown on the spot. This garden, by the way, is one remaining from the five hundred Sansovino counted in his time in Venice.

Gore Vidal claims lineage to the namesake of this little *campo* (and laments that the adjoining canal, Rio di San Vidal, is nowadays too often littered with trash). If the view across the Grand Canal looks slightly familiar, it may be that you have seen it in Canaletto's *Stonemason's Yard*, painted in the early eighteenth century. Of course, the bridge is in place now and the bell tower he depicted fell in 1744, destroying the two houses in front of it. But the house to the right is still with us, as is the church across the way, which has become the home of the Accademia.

Canaletto was about thirty-two when he painted *The Stonemason's Yard* (it has been part of London's National Gallery collection since the early 1800s). It is one of his best-loved artworks from his long and prolific career.

By now, you hear it for sure: the sound of footsteps on heavy wooden planks. It's an unusual sound in a city

so thoroughly paved in cobblestone, marble, and terrazzo. Perhaps that's another reason why the Venetians chose to keep **Ponte dell'Accademia.** It was built by Eugenio Miozzi in 1932 as a temporary replacement for the small, ugly iron bridge occupying Austrians had erected in 1854 so that their troops could be more efficiently deployed throughout the city to quell any uprisings against their rule.

The iron bridge was installed at the same time as Ponte degli Scalzi near the train station, and the architect of both neglected to design the bridges high enough to let *vaporetti* pass underneath. It took eighty years to rectify the problem.

Venetians are usually averse to modern intrusions on the cityscape—particularly along the Grand Canal—but not this time. Maybe they liked the way the wooden bridge evoked the deep, resonant sounds of ship decks and piers from centuries past. Certainly, they enjoyed the easy access across the Grand Canal and no longer wanted to interrupt the flow of pedestrian traffic. In any case, they never did replace this "temporary" bridge with an even more massive one of stone, as had been intended originally. Those plans seem to have been long forgotten, and that's just as well with us.

Refurbished in the mid-1980s, the Accademia Bridge is a permanent fixture in Venice. The views up and down **Canal Grande** make this one of the city's most scenic locations. Facing east toward the Bacino di San Marco, St. Mark's Basin, the first palace on our left is the aforementioned **Ca' Franchetti,** whose owner bequeathed the Ca' d'Oro (Walk 4) with all its art treasures to the state, then moved here and renovated the place in neo-Gothic style in 1896.

The paired palaces next to the Ca' Franchetti were built by the Barbaro family in the fifteenth century and bought by a family named Curtis in the nineteenth century. Henry James stayed here many times and honored his hosts by setting Milly Theale's climactic scenes in *The*

Wings of the Dove at **Pallazzo Barbaro.** The little red house just beyond the second canal is **Casina de Rose.** Antonio Canova had his sculpture studio here in the 1770s, and the pyrotechnic poet Gabriele D'Annunzio lived here during World War I. Its next-door neighbor is **Palazzo Corner**, which was built in the sixteenth century after a design by Sansovino; it is police headquarters now.

Farthest down the Canal on the right, we see **Punta della Dogana,** where the Customhouse still stands, although no longer used today. Later in this walk, we will stand there and take in the magnificent views of the water and St. Mark's before strolling back in this direction to visit Baldassare Longhena's beautiful **Basilica di Santa Maria della Salute** and the single-story **Palazzo Venier dei Leoni,** where Peggy Guggenheim's modern art collection is exhibited.

Along the Canal in the direction of Ponte Rialto and the train station, the farthest palace we see on the left is **Ca' Rezzonico,** which was purchased by Pen Browning in 1887 and where his father, the English poet Robert Browning, died two years later. The building was acquired by the City of Venice in 1935 and converted into the **Museum of Eighteenth-Century Venice** (open 10:00–16:00).

For anyone interested in an independent tour of Ca' Rezzonico, you will find it furnished with pieces from the 1700s. It gives a good example of how a palace must have looked more than two hundred years ago. The ceiling paintings by Giovanni Battista Tiepolo are among the finest of their time. The third floor features paintings by Canaletto, Francesco Guardi, and the largest collection in the world of paintings by Pietro Longhi. A set of frescoes have been relocated here from the house of the Tiepolo family which Gian Domenico created for the family's enjoyment. In this museum you will find also a series of delightful pastel portraits and miniatures by Rosalba Carriera, whom we are about to meet in the Accademia di Belle Arti.

Just beyond Ca' Rezzonico are two fifteenth-century palaces once owned by the Giustiniani family. Wagner spent the winter of 1858–1859 here and wrote *Tristan und Isolde*, deriving inspiration from the gondoliers' calls echoing along the Canal.

Walking down the other side of the Accademia Bridge, we bear right (note the café on the left, which is the only one this far down the Canal; you may choose to stop here after completing this walk) and approach the entrance to the **Accademia di Belle Arti,** the Academy of Fine Arts, also known as the Gallery of the Academy (open 9:00–14:00; Sundays 9:00–13:00; summer months 9:00–18:00; tel. 5210577 and 5222247). This is home to the most extensive collection of Venetian art on earth: a unique chance to see the paintings from a specific school as they evolved over four hundred years' time.

At the end of the Republic in the early nineteenth century, Venice found itself with an abundance of artworks from the churches destroyed by Napoleon. So, in 1807, the city created this gallery by converting the Scuola di Carità and the Chiesa di Santa Maria della Carità, refurbishing the façade in neoclassic style. The lunette over the door, depicting the coronation of the Virgin, is from the original church and was done by Bartolomeo Bon in 1445.

For the purposes of this walk, we should limit our time inside to under one hour; many will want to return in the future. Following the chronological order of the halls, we first visit Room 1 at the top of the staircase. Here are works by the fourteenth-century artists Paolo Veneziano, Antonio Vivarini, and Michele Giambono. The ceiling with its carved-wood and gilded angels is a beautiful work by Marco and Francesco Cozzi in 1484. Every section contains a *cherubino* with eight wings. In the center is a painting of the Almighty by Alvise Vivarini.

We walk behind the large Gothic screen at the end of the room and enter a chamber with two enormous paintings of religious subjects by the great masters of the early Renaissance: *The Virgin and Child with Saints*, by Giovanni Bellini, and *The Presentation of Christ in the Temple*, by Vittore Carpaccio. There is also a beautiful painting of the Virgin by Cima da Conegliano; the background depicts the countryside around Asolo. All of the works in this room were executed as altarpieces during the 1490s.

Ascend the little staircase and pass through the hallway to enter Rooms 4 and 5, where the greatest masterpieces of this collection are displayed. *St. George*, one of Andrea Mantegna's only two paintings in Venice, and Piero della Francesca's *St. Jerome with a Donor* hang as exemplary precursors to the new painting that would evolve in Venice. The change in artistic style, the more sophisticated use of light, color, and form, can be seen by comparing the Mantegna and the Piero with the works in this room by Jacopo Bellini, father of Giovanni, the most celebrated artist in the world around 1500. Room 5 features a number of representations of the Virgin and Child, the subject most often produced in the Bellini studio.

Titian and Giorgione worked in Giovanni Bellini's workshop as well. Titian may have lived to be eighty-six years old; Giorgione died very young. During his short career he produced many paintings, but there are only eight authenticated artworks by him in the world today. Two hang in this very room, the most famous of which is *La Tempesta (The Tempest)*. It is a revolutionary painting, because up until this time most master paintings were designed to celebrate God. But in this work we see a vivid depiction of man as a part of Nature: not man as servant to the hereafter, but man on earth, here and now.

The Tempest has been open to many conflicting interpretations since it was painted around 1505–1507. One such interpretation considers the work an illustration for a book published by the fifteenth-century printer Aldo Manuzio, the creator of italics. Entitled *The Dream of Polifilo*, the literary work was a fantasy embellished with artworks attributed to Bellini, Carpaccio, and Giorgione. In executing this painting, Giorgione created form directly with color—without relying on line to define shape; his technique today might be called impressionistic, and it inspired many of the most renowned artists of the nineteenth century, including Monet and Renoir.

Also important is the other Giorgione here: *La Vecchia (The Old Woman)*, also known as *Col Tempo (As Time Goes By)*. Many believe this woman is the same one as in *The Tempest*, only many years older, as suggested by the lock of hair falling from the right-hand side on both faces. Also, both women appear to be turning toward the viewer, a characteristic innovation of the artist's, which provides movement, personality, and life to each figure.

We exit through Room 3, enter Room 6, and take the first doorway on the right into Room 7, where Lorenzo Lotto's sixteenth-century *Portrait of a Young Gentleman* hangs. Here is the "new man" of the Renaissance, young, peaceful, contemplative, and confident, more concerned with his present life on earth than his future in the hereafter. (You may recognize this work as the one on the cover of the Accademia's catalogue.) We should note that Lotto's career was severely inhibited by Titian's jealousy of his talent. Lotto had to do most of his work outside of Venice.

Back in Room 6, before ascending the four steps into Room 10, we stop for a brief visit with Titian's *St. John the Baptist* (1550). This painting gives us the chance to appreciate the effect that age has had on this and all the works around us. Titian used a color commonly known as Venetian green, a compound of pigments whose principle element was copper resin. Over time, this substance tends to turn black or brown. Consequently, the blues in the *St. John* are no longer balanced by the greens as was originally intended. In Titian's time, the painting was much more vibrant than it is today. Still, it is a fine example of his work.

Entering the gallery's largest room (10), we appreciate

Winged lion atop flagpole in Piazza San Marco

the incredible wealth of old Venice as indicated by the opulent, huge-scale artworks we see around us. Covering the entire wall on the right, Paolo Veronese's *Supper in the House of Levi* (1573) is a massive composition created for the refectory of the Monastero di Santi Giovanni e Paolo. It was originally entitled *The Last Supper*, although it celebrates the lavish life of Venice in the sixteenth century. The artist found himself called before the infamous and dreaded Inquisition for his allegedly sacrilegious use of dwarves, German soldiers, and animals in a holy scene. Veronese attempted to defend himself by pleading for artistic freedom, but he was severely chastised. Facing excommunication or worse, he cleverly extricated himself, not by changing the painting itself, but merely by changing its title and removing its religious significance.

Recent restoration has made it possible to see the exceptional use of color and the exquisite attention to the details of everday life. The costumes of Veronese's characters are particularly noteworthy: they reflect the styles and exotic fabrics worn during the artist's time.

In this room we also find Tintoretto's paintings of episodes involving St. Mark. *The Transportation of the Body of St. Mark* is perhaps the most successful depiction of the event ever created. The natural attitudes of his figures catch us up in the solemnity of the act itself and hold us in the dramatic moment.

Titian's last work, the impressionistic *Pietà*, graces this room with its presence. By this late stage in his career, with his eyesight failing, Titian "painted much more with his fingers than his brush," the painter Jacopo Palma the Younger (Palma Giovane) wrote of the master. Studying it closely, we can see the heavy brushwork and streaks of color to which Palma referred. Titian died before he completed the painting; Palma completed it.

In Room 11, the seventeenth-century *Martyrdom of St. Peter*, by Luca Giordano, is the last on the left. Opposite that is *The Last Supper*, by the Genoese Bernardo Strozzi, who was strongly influenced by Rubens. Veronese's *Annunciation* is worthy of note. And the large round painting by Giovanni Battista Tiepolo, *The Invention of the Cross* (1743–1745), pays quiet homage to Veronese. Tiepolo drew from the earlier artist when decorating the ceilings of churches and palaces, especially in his use of colors.

Exit through the door on the left, pass through the long corridor, and go through the first door on the left to Room 17. Paintings by Canaletto, Francesco Guardi, and Pietro Longhi are exhibited here. In the inner chamber are a notable set of pastel portraits by Rosalba Carriera (1675–1758), unique for their era because they were done by a woman, who sold her portraits for twice the price of Canaletto's oils. Carriera's career must have been truly inspirational. See if you can find her self-portrait among the group portrait of the Leblonde family. Also note the lovely *Portrait of Anne Charlotte Gauthier de Loiserolle*.

After returning to the long corridor, we make two lefts in Room 18 to enter Room 19. From here, we enter Room 20 on the left. The paintings here come from the Scuola Grande di San Giovanni Evangelista and celebrate the miraculous cross it possessed. Two large representations by Gentile Bellini, dated around 1497–1500, are concerned with the cross: *The Miracle of the Cross in St. Mark's Square* and *The Miracle of the Cross*. Vittore Carpaccio's *Miracle of the True Cross* takes place at the old wooden Rialto Bridge, which we discussed in Walk 2. (Interesting here is a depiction of Jewish merchants wearing their distinctive hats.)

Exit Room 20 and turn left; on the right is Room 21, adorned with the works of Vittore Carpaccio (1460–1526), which were commissioned by a minor *scuola*, Santa Orsola (St. Ursula). Among them is *The Legend of St. Ursula*, dated 1491. With this painting, Carpaccio emerged as a mature artist with admirable skills of originality, organization, narration, and a wonderful command of light. The naturalistic genre scene of *The Dream of St. Ursula* is one of the most popular of Venetian paintings.

We go back to Room 19, turn left, and proceed down two staircases to Room 24, where we find the very theatrical *Presentation in the Temple* by Titian. This is one of the artist's best works, completed around 1534–1538. The event depicted would have taken place in the century before Christ, but the figures wear Venetian fashion of the sixteenth century. Elegant ladies play with a dog as two elderly people—a woman selling chickens and eggs, and a man reclining on the staircase—go about their normal routines, seemingly unaware of the event taking place around them.

Exit through the door on the left under the painting and return to Room 1. The exit from the building is down the stairs.

After stepping outside, move left and follow Rio Terrà della Carità. (For future reference: If you take the little street on the right between the photocopying shop and the furniture store, a few paces ahead, you'll find **El Souk**, as close to a traditional English pub as you'll find in Venice. Dark, intimate, and friendly, it plays popular music for its customers, who nestle into the cozy banquettes all around the room. El Souk specializes in "American cocktails" and English brews such as Guinness and Tennent's. The owner is named Franco.

At night, the place is Americanized a bit and the little dance floor off to the side is opened up. The music gets louder as the younger set packs in to dance. Night spots like this are a rarity in Venice, so if you find yourself in the mood for this type of entertainment, remember its location and come back after eight or nine o'clock.

Still on the Rio Terà della Carità, pass Campiello Calbo on the right and keep walking straight ahead along and toward the back of the Accademia. There you may discover a family of scraggly cats waiting for you in an overgrown garden. Turn right on Calle Larga Nani, then left onto Fondamenta Nani, and proceed alongside the canal.

(Almost immediately to the left is a little shop where you'll find a fine selection of wines at very good prices, many of which you can sample at the bar.)

You may choose later to cross the nearest bridge and visit the church, but first walk past it to the left to see a gondola workshop, **Squero di San Trovaso,** from across the waterway. (Oh, by the way, in building no. 944 right beside you, above the "Trasporti" sign, Ezra Pound used to live on the top floor. "Where [the *rio*] Ogni Santi meets San Trovaso things have ends and beginnings," Pound wrote of this site.)

And some "things" unique to Venice still have their beginnings right here today. Gondolas are fashioned by hand in the little boatyard across the canal.

Surrounded by old Venetian stone and stucco, the gondola shop is in a storybook setting, with two-story dark-wood structures and the shock of red geraniums in balcony-railing flower boxes. Laundry flutters on the line. An old ladder leans against the house, a pile of paint-splattered sawhorses nearby. And the sounds of the work done here seem serious and solid.

The man who builds gondolas here is the near-legendary Maestro Gastone Di Nardo, hardy and skillful, humble and proud. Not yet sixty, he is the youngest of only three men currently carrying on the ancient traditions of gondola building. With his nephews and apprentices, he creates the oldest type of boat in the Venetian Lagoon.

The gondola was first mentioned in literature in 697. And the methods of its fabrication have changed very little over the last thirteen hundred years. Traditionally built of 280 different pieces of eight types of wood (including the walnut oarlock, the *forcola*), the boat has a flat bottom and no keel to facilitate turning around sharp corners in the shallow waters of the canals.

All construction is accomplished by hand. In the studio to the left, every piece of a gondola is cut and shaped, hewn and finished using tools a hundred generations old. Once the skeletal structure is completed, the wood for

the sides is heated on open fires until the ingrained mois-
ture is turned to steam and each piece can be bent into
place. The characteristic glossy black finish is painstak-
ingly applied in the shed to the right. The entire process
is time-consuming; it takes about 6,000 hours to complete one gondola. If proper care is taken in maintaining
the craft, a gondola will last for generations.

Every gondola is 10.15 meters (33 feet, 3 inches) long
and 1.4 meters (4 feet, 6 inches) wide and weighs 700
kilograms (1,540 pounds). A six-pronged *ferro* (one prong
for each of Venice's districts, *sestieri*) adorns the bow.
Besides its decorative purpose, the heavy metal prow-
piece helps to counterbalance the weight of the gondolier
and keeps the boat riding flat in the water.

If you look down the entire length of a gondola, you
will see that its body is asymmetrical, bending more on
the left than the right. This design element compensates
for the side thrust of the oar and the weight of the boatman, who stands to the back left.

During the sixteenth century, some 10,000 gondolas
floated through Venice's canals. Fewer than 500 are in
use today. Once they were decorated in every color imag-
inable and their passengers were protected from the elements with an elaborate canopy known as a *felze*. The
plague of 1562 brought a government decree that all gondolas be painted black, and they have stayed this way
ever since. Many of the boats were used to ferry the dead,
and it was felt they should be more somber. Years after
the plague, the government kept the decree on the books
as a means of cutting down on private citizens' displays
of ostentation. (It remained as one of their sumptuary
laws, which attempted to control the public's wearing of
certain jewelry and fine materials as well. In Venice, remember, only the Republic could strut its stuff.) Modern
legend, however, has it that Peggy Guggenheim, whom
we will meet at the end of this walk, painted her private
gondola purple!

It costs about $30,000 to purchase a new, standard-

model gondola nowadays. Optional detailing, upholstery, and adornments can bring the price thousands of dollars above that. Upkeep is expensive as well. Every couple of months, the boat must be brought back to the *squero*, where it is pulled from the water, tilted on its side, cleaned, recaulked, and resurfaced with a special green copper-based paint that helps prevent a buildup of algae, which adds drag and weight to the craft and slows it down.

The refitting work being done on a gondola as you stand here just might be on a gondola belonging to our friend Luciano Santini, one of Venice's more colorful and engaging gondoliers. He comes here often—he and the Maestro have known each other all their lives—and together they apply great care in maintaining the graceful gondola that Luciano has named *Margherita*, after his mother.

For all its romance, the life of a gondolier is strenuous and sometimes quite dangerous. He must stand for eight to twelve hours a day, in all types of weather, continually rocked by waves. With every stroke of his oar, he propels a ton's worth of boat and passengers, all the while negotiating mazelike courses choked with all sorts of traffic, some of which could cut his gondola in two if he weren't so skillful at maneuvering.

A gondolier's average income is comfortably middle-class. The city government regulates his rates, so it's really up to him to make what he can of his career. Still, many tourists nowadays decide that the service he provides is just too expensive (around $60 for a fifty-minute ride). What a shame! Among the categories of once-in-a-lifetime experiences, a ride in a gondola is well worth the price.

To become a gondolier, one must be a son or nephew of a gondolier. There are fewer than four hundred licenses issued at any one time; most of those licenses are held for a lifetime. So competition for any new openings in the gondolier business is stiff; the job is demanding and requires dedication. The "exam" each applicant must complete successfully before he is eligible for a license is extensive and calls for thorough mastery of the craft, comprehensive knowledge of the canals and historical sites, fluency in two or more languages, and a temperament that is friendly, gracious, and understanding. These men are the true hosts of Venice, the keepers of a tradition that is nearly sixty generations old. May they always grace the waters of this city with their unique presence. Gentlemen, *salute!*

If you'd like to tour the Chiesa di San Trovaso, follow these next few paragraphs. If not, just walk straight ahead to the Zattere and read a couple of pages about the church along the way.

Backtracking just a bit along the *fondamenta*, cross the nearest bridge and enter Campo di San Trovaso. The **Chiesa di San Trovaso** derives its name from the two saints, Gervasio and Protasio, to whom it is dedicated.

Tradition holds that the church has two façades, because its site marks the boundary between two rival neighborhood factions in ancient Venice, the Castellani and the Nicolotti, who vented their competitiveness by staging annual regattas instead of the violent street brawls and pitched battles on bridges that so many other districts fostered. Whenever a wedding took place at this church involving members from both factions, the Castellani used the south door and the Nicolotti the portal to the west.

Inside, Tintoretto's *Last Supper* hangs on the right wall of the Chapel of the Sacrament, and his *Temptation of St. Anthony* can be found in the chapel to the left of the high altar. In the chapel on the other side of the chancel is Michele Giambono's *St. Chrisogono*. The saint appears elegantly mounted on his steed in fifteenth-century knightly fashion in this, one of the finest Gothic paintings in Venice.

Exit the church and cross the elevated *campo*. It is raised by containers of clay under the pavement, which were used to filter and purify rainwater collected for the well. Many *campi* in Venice are elevated above street level for another reason: they are the site of old church cemeteries. (The little burial sites had filled up many times over by the time Napoleon took control of Venice in 1797. He solved the problem by creating the Cimitero di San Michele, the huge island cemetery that we will see in the distance during Walk 4.)

Cross the little bridge straight ahead, turn left and then right, and head for the water. Here turn left, cross over the bridge, and step onto **Fondamenta delle Zattere.** This long, sunny southern promenade is so named for the timber rafts, *zattere*, that used to be floated in from the mainland and moored on this side of the **Canale della Giudecca.** Facing the water, we turn left.

Today, the restaurants along the water continue the tradition by extending outdoor seating areas over the waves. Any one of them is a nice place to sit and enjoy some refreshment. Of the two spots for ice cream and coffee we see nearby, **Da Nico** is preferred; its *gelato*, particularly the chocolate and fruit-flavored, is superb.

Across the water, we see the **Giudecca,** the island on which Michelangelo sought solace and solitude during his exile from Florence in 1529. (The artist had been named chief military engineer in charge of fortifications by the Republic of Florence during a war involving Pope Clement VII, Holy Roman Emperor Charles V, and the French king, Francis I. This was a no-win situation, and once the fighting stopped, Michelangelo was forced to skip town for a couple of months and wait for things to cool down.) Contrary to popular belief, the island's name does not have anything to do with the Jews, who have lived in Venice for nine hundred years; possibly it comes from the term *giudicato*, meaning "judged": banished conspirators were forced to cross the canal separating the island from Venice.

Just ahead on the left we find the **Chiesa di Santa Maria del Rosario,** commonly known as the **Chiesa dei Gesuati** (open 8:00–12:00 and 17:00–19:00), one of the finest examples of Venetian late Baroque decoration. It is unique to Venice for its rich green-and-white marble motifs that look like damask wall hangings. The high windows flood the space with light and give a feeling of warmth and radiance.

Taken over by the Jesuits in 1657, the church was redesigned by Domenico Rossi in 1729 on the plan of a Latin cross with a single nave and side chapels. It is dedicated to the Virgin Mary (of the Rosary) and glorifies particularly her Assumption. Giovanni Battista Tiepolo decorated the ceilings and the monochrome lunettes in 1739. A Crucifixion by Tintoretto, dated 1560, hangs at the third altar on the left.

At the corner of Campiello della Calcina and before the *ponte* spanning Rio di San Vio is the little pink *pensione* known as La Calcina, where John Ruskin lived. His room was just over the portico overlooking the Giudecca Canal. It is claimed that he wrote much of *The Stones of Venice* while ensconced here in 1877. Others insist it was *St. Mark's Rest* that he worked on during his stay. Still others believe that by this point in his career, Ruskin suffered from serious, chronic bouts of depression and delusion and did very little writing at all. Another little footnote: The Venetian poet-scholar Apostolo Zeno died here in 1750 at the age of eighty.

The name of the next bridge over Rio delle Torresette, Ponte agli Incurabili ("incurables"), refers to what was once a nearby hospital and is today a rehabilitation center for juvenile delinquents. (Yes, believe it or not, even Venice has such problems.)

Across the water, we see the **Chiesa del Redentore**, the Church of the Redeemer (open 7:00–12:00 and 15:30–19:30), one of the finest examples of work in Venice by the sixteenth-century architect Andrea Palladio.

Born on November 30, 1508, Andrea di Pietro della Gondola grew up in a mainland village near Padua and, at the age of fifteen, was apprenticed to a stonemason in Vicenza. He was a conscientious worker and a quick student, but it was his personable wit and facility with mathematics that caught the eye of the patron/humanist/ scholar/poet Giovanni Giorgio Trissino, who became the young man's mentor in 1536.

Trissino gave Andrea the affectionate nickname "Palladio" after Pallas, the angel of wisdom in his poem *L'Italia Liberata dai Goti*, who explains the significance of geometrical proportions in architecture. It would appear that Trissino set out to make this nickname a self-fulfilling prophecy, because he took Andrea to Rome in 1545 and introduced the young man to the world of classical thought as outlined by the Roman architectural theorist Vitruvius.

In the sixteenth century, it was believed that mathematics and music were intrinsically related and that a study of this relationship would reveal certain laws governing artistic proportion. In music it was known that if two strings, one half the length of the other (1:2), were plucked, their pitch would be one octave apart. Similar relationships were established for the musical fifth (2:3) and fourth (3:4). And architects therefore held that if a room's width equaled one-half, two-thirds, or three-quarters its length, its aesthetic appeal would be likewise harmonious.

Palladio took these principles of mathematics and music a step further to include ratios involving the major and minor third, major and minor sixth, and so on.

Inspired by this new knowledge, Palladio returned to the Veneto, where he established himself as the preeminent designer of country villas for the Venetian ruling class. His legacy to architecture is most richly evident among the rolling hills in and around Vicenza; the entire city seems a museum to his talent. Most important among his sponsors there were the brothers Daniele and Marcantonio Barbaro, who commissioned Palladio's most important works, including the Villa Barbaro Maser in Asolo.

Palladio arrived in Venice in 1560, just as Sansovino was nearing the end of his career. Palladio immediately set about distinguishing his work from the masters of the era by drawing from the classical principles he'd learned while in Rome.

After Sansovino's death in 1570, Palladio became the chief architect of the Republic. In that same year, he published his *Quattro Libri dell'Architettura* (*Four Books of Architecture*), in which he expounded his principles; these had their most profound effect on English, French, and American architecture of the eighteenth century. (Interestingly, mainly Protestant cultures embraced these theories inspired by ancient Rome, over those of Catholic Italy. The Vatican adhered to its own theories on architecture, which pretty much peaked during the Renaissance.) Nevertheless, Palladio's literary work was a tremendous success. Fourteen editions of his *Four Books* were published in English alone between 1663 and 1738.

Thomas Jefferson owned a copy of this work and referred to it as his bible while he designed his home at Monticello and the campus of the University of Virginia. It is important to note that Jefferson thoroughly absorbed Palladio's philosophical and intellectual social models. He envisioned Virginia as a New World version of Venetian society.

In 1576, Venice was struck by a hideous eighteen-month-long bubonic plague which claimed 51,000 lives, a third of the city's population. The following year, the government commissioned Palladio to construct a votive temple consecrated to Christ, their Redeemer. To overwhelming approval, he unveiled his designs for the Chiesa del Redentore.

The church's façade presents three triangular pediments borrowed from designs of pagan Greek temples of antiquity. Their combined effect is a dramatic, forced three-dimensionality that unites the building's exterior to the proportions of its interior.

Palladio died on August 19, 1580, twelve years before the completion of the Redentore; Antonio da Ponte took over the task. No doubt Palladio would be pleased to know that the church has been well loved and well utilized over the centuries.

Every third Saturday in July, for the Feast of the Redeemer, Venetians celebrate their deliverance from that plague by building a bridge of rafts across the Giudecca Canal. In the evening, practically every craft available ventures out into the water and a huge fireworks display is launched from the Bacino di San Marco. As the last burst of color dissolves into the night sky, a second incendiary extravaganza is set off from another direction, from the island of San Giorgio.

Throughout it all, tens of thousands of Venetians eat and drink and sing away the night on the water. Tradition dictates that the hardiest of the revelers then make their way to the Lido to watch the sun come up over the Adriatic. Throughout the next morning and afternoon, a constant stream of (hung over) celebrants crosses the floating bridge and visits the church to give thanks for their salvation.

Toward the end of the *fondamenta*, we pass the warehouses where, until the eighteenth century, precious Venetian salt was stored for export. It's hard to believe in this day and age that a substance as common as salt could have ever been worth twice its weight in gold. But before Venice started processing salt on a mass-market basis, the inland populace was starved for the stuff and was willing to pay a fortune for it. Not only for use on the table and in the kitchen, but also as a preservative for fish and meats, salt was unsurpassed. Many a family survived each year's leaner months because of the salt-cured protein they were able to keep at hand.

In a few dozen yards, we reach **Punta della Dogana**, Customhouse Point, at the mouth of the Grand Canal. Here we discover one of the most dramatic views of the city's harbor.

Designed by Giuseppe Benoni in 1672, the Customhouse was where visitors to Venice first arrived to present their credentials, state their business, and prove their financial viability before being allowed to enter the heart of the city across the water. And it was from this point that a huge iron chain was stretched across the Grand

Canal whenever Venice was threatened with invasion by hostile forces.

Like the Statue of Liberty in New York Harbor, the statue of Fortune greets us as it has greeted all arrivals from atop the golden globe overhead. This huge weathervane is actually a symbolic kinetic sculpture: appropriately, fickle Fate continues to be blown this way and that by chance winds.

Across the water to the right, we see the **Basilica di San Giorgio Maggiore,** the other major accomplishment in Venice by Andrea Palladio. The island on which the church sits was once the site of a Benedictine monastery. The old cloisters are today the home of one of the most important cultural centers in the world, Fondazione Cini. The foundation maintains a library and documentation center for the history of music and the visual arts. The island is used also for meetings and seminars of scholars and diplomats, the most important recently being the 1978 and 1986 summits of the eight leading countries of the world.

Walking back up the Canal Grande, we soon reach the **Basilica di Santa Maria della Salute** (open 8:00–12:00 and 15:00–18:00), an impressive structure also commissioned by the government. The church was built in thanksgiving to the Virgin, the bringer of health, *salute,* for Venice's deliverance from yet another devastating plague that struck in 1630. It is recorded that 595 people died one November day alone. In sixteen months, 46,490 had fallen victim to the disease. Understandably, the survivors had good cause to be grateful for its end.

Built atop 1,156,627 pylons, the Baroque church was designed by Baldassare Longhena. He described it as "a virgin work, never seen before, strange, worthy, and beautiful, in the shape of a round 'machine' such as had never been seen, or invented either in its whole or in part [in] any other church in this city." The architect died five years before its completion in 1687. Symbolically, the Salute is at the midpoint of the semicircle formed between the Redentore and St. Mark's main altar.

On the façade are a dozen columnar scrolls, where statues of the apostles stand tall. The fifteen steps leading to the main entrance evoke those of the Temple of Solomon in Jerusalem, site of the Presentation of the Virgin.

We enter through the side doors and go to the sacristy, to the left of the main altar. Titian's *St. Mark Enthroned with Sts. Sebastian, Roch, Cosmas, and Damian* (1511) adorns the wall there with a fresh and youthful luminosity. Among the numerous artworks exhibited in the church, there are three others by Titian: *The Sacrifice of Abraham, David and Goliath,* and *Cain and Abel* (1540–1549). A very important painting by Tintoretto, *The Marriage at Cana* (1551), is also here.

On November 21 every year, on the Feast of the Presentation of the Virgin, another raft bridge is constructed across the Grand Canal from the church of Santa Maria del Giglio and the front doors of the Salute are thrown open. Across this bridge come Venetians with offerings of thanksgiving to the Virgin for saving their ancestors from the dreaded plague.

After exiting the church, we bear left and cross the first wood-and-stone bridge, Ponte de l'Abazia. The building on the left houses studios and laboratories for restoring Venice's many paintings in need of such work.

Cross Campo San Gregorio, on the right side of which is the glass factory of a Murano-based company, **Cenedese**. In a three-floor palace, glassware is displayed in rooms overlooking the Grand Canal. Continue along, following signs reading "Guggenheim Collection." (The *traghetto* that stops nearby crosses the Canal to the Hotel Gritti Palace and is the quickest way to return to Piazza San Marco at the completion of this walk.)

Cross Ponte San Gregorio, walk along Ramo Barbaro into Campiello Barbaro. Cross Ponte San Cristofolo and proceed ahead along the *calle* to the **Peggy Guggenheim Collection** (open 11:00–18:00; Saturdays 18:00–21:00; closed Tuesdays).

In 1949, the great, adventuresome, and eccentric patron of modern art, Peggy Guggenheim (whom Gore Vidal has described as "the last of Henry James's transatlantic heroines") purchased the unfinished eighteenth-century **Palazzo Venier dei Leoni**. With characteristic flair and élan, she made it her home; filled it with her extensive collection of artworks by the likes of Pablo Picasso, Alexander Calder, Jackson Pollock (her most notable discovery), Max Ernst (whom she married), Paul Klee, Marc Chagall, and Salvador Dalí; and promptly opened her doors to the public. Her lifelong mission to promote and present art of the twentieth century has resulted in one of the most important collections of modern art in Europe.

The welded iron gates you see here were made in 1961 by Claire Falkenstein, who incorporated pieces of Murano glass into the design. Beyond them is one of the oldest, largest, and grandest gardens in all of Venice: a treasure unto itself and a refreshing spot to rest, amid greenery and beneath shady umbrella pines. Legend holds that the Venier family once kept lions in the garden, hence the "dei Leoni" in the name of the palazzo. And Peggy Guggenheim, Venice's patron saint of modern art, who died in December 1979, is buried in this garden.

Among the hundreds of artworks here, Marino Marini's *Angel of the Citadel* can be found just outside the main entrance, in the little courtyard atop the staircase leading up from the Canal. This joyous bronze statue of a naked man on a neighing horse, his arms—and erection—fully outstretched, welcomes all who visit with unabashed enthusiasm. The statue is an appropriate symbol of the way Peggy Guggenheim embraced all of life. (Marini cast this statue with a threaded phallus which could be unscrewed and removed whenever nuns or other sensitive visitors arrive to view the collection. If it's missing when you're here, you're amid very select company!)

With this visit to the Guggenheim Collection, we complete Walk 3. You may wish to take the *traghetto* we mentioned earlier to cross the Canal, or you may choose to follow the signs back over Ponte dell'Accademia.

Walk · 4

Doges, Priests, and Jews

TO THE GHETTO

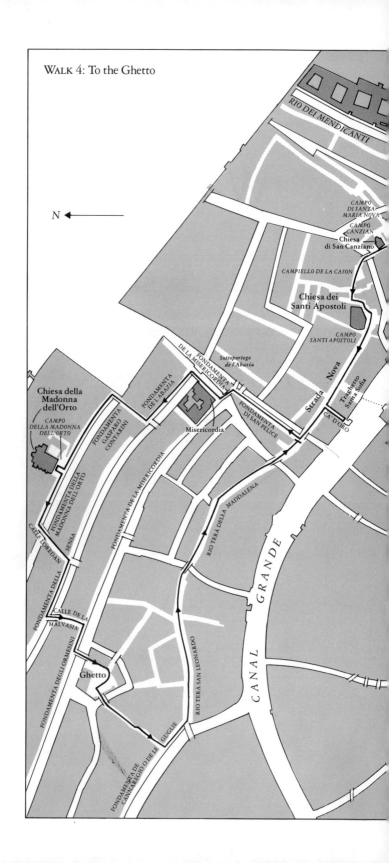

WALK 4: To the Ghetto

N ←

RIO DEI MENDICANTI

CAMPO DI SANTA MARIA NOVA
CAMPO CANZIAN
Chiesa di San Canziano

CAMPIELLO DE LA CASON

Chiesa dei Santi Apostoli

CAMPO SANTI APOSTOLI

FONDAMENTA DE LA MISERICORDIA
Sottoportego de l'Abazia

FONDAMENTA DE LA ABAZIA

Chiesa della Madonna dell'Orto

CAMPO DELLA MADONNA DELL'ORTO

FONDAMENTA GASPARO CONTARINI

Misericordia

FONDAMENTA DI SAN FELICE

Strada Nova

Traghetto Santa Sofia

CA' D'ORO

FONDAMENTA DELLA MADONNA DELL'ORTO

SENSA

FONDAMENTA DE LA MISERICORDIA

RIO TERA DELLA MADDALENA

CALLE TOREDAN

FONDAMENTA DELLA

CALLE DE LA MALVASIA

FONDAMENTA DEGLI ORMESINI

Ghetto

RIO TERA SAN LEONARDO

CANAL GRANDE

FONDAMENTA DE CANNAREGIO O DE LE GUGLIE

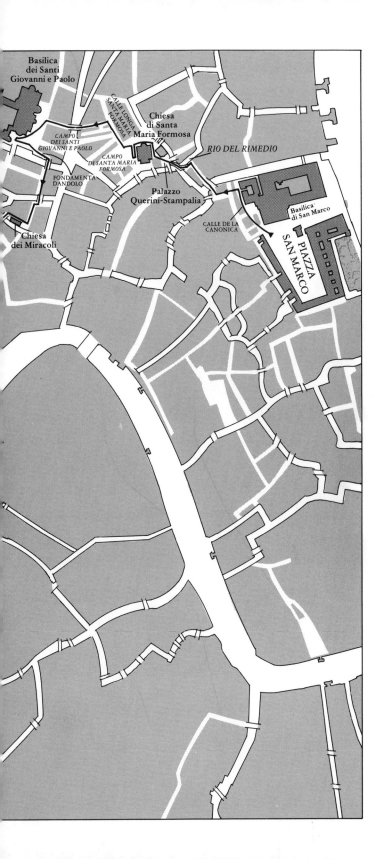

Starting Point: Piazza San Marco

This walk can be made between either 9:00 and 12:30 or 14:30 and 18:00. You'll have to keep up a pretty good pace to cover it in three hours. The Ca' d'Oro is open only in the morning, and certain Ghetto sites are closed on Friday after-noons, all day Saturday, and on Jewish religious holidays.

It is in remembrance of things past that we return to this Piazza. Gone are the religious processions and political pageants that once filled the square with awesome splendor. Gone, too, are the summer-night gatherings when tens of thousands of Venetians sat at long tables and played *lotto* until the wee hours of the morning. And once, in his youth, one of the writers of this book, called Sandro for short, picked up his grandmother's winning card and ran around the crowded space amid thunderous applause to collect his prize.

Gone from this city are many of the quainter customs among its people, such as the early-spring evenings when families of neighbors carried chairs from their homes and sat in nearby *campi* to witness the annual burning of "The Old Lady," winter's straw-filled effigy, as children sang and danced around the flames and celebrated the close of the cold and dreary months.

Time was, on hot summer days, the sky over the Lido was abuzz with biplanes that sprinkled the air with tiny parachutes filled with candies for the children below. And while you can still find many adults in Venice who recall with fondness the taste of chocolate laced with saltwater, these too are only memories, because this custom is gone as well.

Remaining with us are the grander, more commercial international festivals of music, film, and art. And while so much of traditional Venetian life is preserved for us in the present, so much of it has faded into the past.

Carnevale, Carnival, still brings thousands of celebrants to Venice every February. During the three weeks before Lent, Venetian days and nights are filled with costume balls and concerts, feasts and parades, street theater and art exhibits, outdoor dances and circus acts. Masks and elaborate dress are de rigueur as all of Venice colorfully cloaks itself in festive mystery and the city is enshrouded by gray winter fog. In recent years, Carnival events have been staged in *campi* all over the city to take the strain off Piazza San Marco. But the grand finale, on *Martedì Grasso*, "Fat Tuesday" before Ash Wednesday, is always staged right here in the Piazza.

As in Walk 1, exit Piazzetta dei Leoni via Calle de la Canonica, but take the last left before the bridge onto Ramo va in Canonica. Duck under the "Grotta Music" sign, and turn right onto Ramo de l'Anzolo. Cross Ponte del Rimedio and proceed along Calle del Rimedio, then move left on the *fondamenta* along Rio del Rimedio. You might wish to stop on Ponte Pasqualigo e Avogardo to take in the view. From this bridge you can see a total of ten *ponti*, more than from any other bridge in the city.

Enter Campiello Querini-Stampalia, proceed to the right, and cross the third bridge, a small one of wood and iron, from which you enter the **Palazzo Querini-Stampalia** (open 10:00–12:30), once the home of a powerful family with a long and checkered history in Venice.

Toward the beginning of Walk 2, we learned the story of Baiamonte Tiepolo's ill-fated insurrection against Doge

Pietro Gradenigo in 1310. One branch of the Querini family, headed by the brothers Marco and Piero, allied themselves with Tiepolo; when he was captured, tried, and exiled for treasonous activities against the Republic, so too were they. This, however, didn't seem to crimp their style very much, because they quickly conquered the Aegean island of Stampalia and added its name to theirs.

The other branch of the Querini clan, headed by a third brother, Giovanni, remained behind in Venice, prospered for more than five centuries, and distinguished themselves as noble statesmen and warriors for the Republic.

Upon his death on December 11, 1868, the original Giovanni's namesake Count Giovanni Querini-Stampalia bequeathed to the state his extensive library and considerable art collection, which is still open to the public. Today, scholars and students who visit the palace's first floor enjoy access to some 150,000 published volumes, 1,300 manuscripts, and countless newspapers, journals, essays, and pamphlets written between the fourteenth and mid-nineteenth centuries.

The second floor of the palace has been preserved pretty much as the count left it. Many rooms are decorated with the original furnishings and give us a chance to see how one family must have lived a century and more ago.

The extensive art collection is devoted primarily to paintings of scenes from Venetian life. There are works by Giovanni Bellini and Giovanni Battista Tiepolo, and one room holds sixty-nine paintings by Gabriel Bella.

Certainly a lesser talent than Bellini and Tiepolo, Bella is nevertheless worthy of our appreciation. He is the Venetian artist who recorded every public religious and political festival that regularly took place in Venice during the eighteenth century. Scenes of bullfights, gondola races, regattas, bridge fights between *sestieri*, religious processions, Carnival and other holiday celebrations, gambling games, opera performances, and political receptions are captured and displayed in a sort of time capsule of Venetian life of the era. It is easy to see how Venice became the Disneyland of its day, with a major spectacle happening nearly every week.

If we exit the *campiello* to the right, the **Chiesa di Santa Maria Formosa** (open 8:30–12:30 and 16:30–18:30) is straight ahead of us. Enter through the side doors; if they are locked, walk around to the front.

The original church was built in the seventh century, according to popular legend by San Magno (Magnus), bishop of Oderzo. Actually, this is one of eight churches he constructed after the Madonna appeared to him in the form of a beautiful and buxom (*formosa*) young woman and commanded him to build a church wherever a white cloud touched the ground.

Venetians have another legend about the original chapel, which began as the oratory of the Scuola dei Casselleri (makers of marriage coffers). It is held that on a summer's morning in 944 a bevy of virgins on their way to the church to be married were abducted by a gang of Slavs, who intended to carry them off to Dalmatia. Just in time, the *casselleri* rescued the young women and saved the (wedding) day. Since then, until the fall of the Republic, the doge made a yearly Candlemas Day visit of thanksgiving to the *scuola*, where he was given a straw hat to protect him from the rain ("But what shall I do if it rains?") and a glass of wine for his thirst ("And what shall I do if I am thirsty?"). You can see one of these straw hats in the Museo Correr (Walk 2) and you might have already seen Bella's painting of the ceremony in Palazzo Querini-Stampalia.

After a remodeling in the eleventh century, the church was rebuilt in 1492 by Mauro Coducci, who patterned it after the central structure of St. Mark's. The two main façades of the church were built with money given by the Capello family. The classical one, facing the canal, was built in 1542 to honor Captain Vincenzo Capello, who defeated the Turks in 1541. His figure on the sarcophagus inside the church is by Pietro Grazioli da Salò, of the Sansovino school. The other façade, built in 1604, includes three portrait busts of members of the Capello family, surmounted by five seventeenth-century statues representing the Virgin and the Virtues.

The interior is a typical example of Coducci's work: a Byzantine/Renaissance plan, with a Latin cross super-imposed on the previous Greek-cross foundation. Slender columns support little cupolas and barrel vaults create an elegant, spacious effect.

The dome was rebuilt in 1668, after an earthquake destroyed part of it, and restored to its original shape in 1921 after being hit by an incendiary bomb five years earlier. During this restoration, frescoes were removed and the round windows in the nave were reopened to the sunlight.

There are three paintings of interest. The first is Jacopo Palma the Elder's painting of St. Barbara, an image of a beautiful and robust Venetian woman, which hangs over the altar in the southern transept of the church. George Eliot wrote of the painting: "An almost unique presentation of a hero woman, standing in calm preparation for the martyrdom without the slightest air of pietism, yet the expression of a mind filled with serious conviction."

To the left of *St. Barbara*, Palma's *St. John the Baptist* reminds us of Giorgione's prototypical young men, and especially of the Sebastiano del Piombo's *St. John the Baptist* in San Giovanni Grisostomo (Walk 2). Palma, a contemporary of Titian, was recognized in his time as worthy of equal note. Not many of his paintings have survived, however, in part because Titian was so adept at eradicating the careers of his competitors.

Of Bartolomeo Vivarini's 1473 altarpiece honoring the Madonna della Misericordia, the Madonna of Mercy, it is documented that the congregation paid for the execution. The figures huddled around the Virgin appear to be portraits of the parish priest and certain select parishioners (undoubtedly the most generous contributors).

The Vivarini family workshop vied with that of the Bellinis as the leading producer of representations of the Virgin Mary. In the scene on the right of the Vivarini altarpiece is an interesting way of showing the interior of a Venetian home in the fifteenth century. The household items and the bottle-glass windows (similar to the upper windows in this very building) were typical of the era.

We exit the church through the front doors and enter Campo di Santa Maria Formosa, traditionally the site of bullfights, and a favorite location for open-air theatrical events. Today, this sunny square is filled with brightly colored stalls selling fruit and vegetables. It is one of the most charming points in the city, where tourists can enjoy everyday life. There are two notable palaces around the square: Palazzo Vittori (No. 5246), whose cross was much touted by Ruskin, and Palazzo Malipiero-Trevisan (No. 5250), a fine sixteenth-century construction by Santo Lombardo.

Walk around the bell tower. At its base is a stone carving of a grotesque head of which John Ruskin wrote: "A head—huge, inhuman and monstrous—leering in bestial degradation, too foul to be either pictured or described, or to be beheld for more than an instant . . . for in that head is embodied the type of the evil spirit to which Venice was abandoned in the fourth period of her decline; and it is well that we should see and feel the full horror of it on this spot, and know what pestilence it was that came and breathed upon her beauty, until it melted away like the white cloud from the ancient fields of Santa Maria Formosa."

Exit the *campo* by way of Calle Longa Santa Maria Formosa, near the clock straight ahead. On this street, the restaurant **Mascaron** (closed Sundays) offers traditional Venetian fare in a serve-yourself style. It is a friendly place, owned by a man nicknamed Gigia, and is an excellent spot for lunch or dinner. Bean soup, spaghetti with all types of sauce, and an excellent house wine are offered at unusually reasonable prices.

Ruskin called him "grotesque"

Follow the yellow sign that directs you to the Basilica di Santi Giovanni e Paolo. Turn left onto Calle Cicogna and cross Ponte Milner. It's beside a pretty black iron bridge near a Y intersection of canals. Straight ahead we walk into Campo Santi Giovanni e Paolo. For all its works of art and historical memories, many consider this the grandest and most important *campo* in Venice.

Directly before us stands the **Monument to Bartolomeo Colleoni**, believed to be one of the finest equestrian statues on earth. (Ruskin once claimed: "I do not believe that there is a more glorious work of sculpture existing in the world.") It's a more than fitting tribute to a "macho man" whose name sounds like *coglioni*, which means "testicles," of which he claimed to have *three*. And until 1866, this was Venice's only outdoor public monument honoring a specific individual.

In his time, Colleoni was a renowned *condottiere*, mercenary leader, who plied his trade for the highest bidder and racked up a most impressive list of victories to his credit. In 1439, he was hired to liberate Brescia from the besieging duke of Milan. This he accomplished by transporting six galleys and twenty smaller ships up the Adige River and *over* Mount Altissimo to Lake Garda. Caught off guard, the Milanese forces were quickly routed and Brescia was saved.

A few years later, he was hired by Milan (apparently, they held no grudges) to defeat the French army of Charles VII, and later still by Florence to drive the Medicis from the city. In 1455, Colleoni returned to Venice, where he was appointed the Republic's commanding general for life; he would hold the position for twenty years while amassing a significant fortune in the process.

On his deathbed in 1475, Colleoni warned Venice against ever granting anyone else so much power ("I could have done so much harm"). His will bequeathed to the Republic his considerable wealth, if a monument in his honor were erected in Piazza San Marco.

This request created quite a dilemma for the city fathers. While they wanted very much to keep Colleoni's fortune, the idea of placing a monument to him in the Piazza was completely against their thinking. (Remember, the Republic did not allow the glorification of any individual, and it certainly would not tolerate a statue in the middle of the state square.) Therefore, a little inventive rationalization was called into play as they decided that the *campo* outside the Scuola Grande di San Marco would be a fitting site for the monument.

Andrea del Verrocchio, teacher of Leonardo da Vinci, was commissioned by the state to design the statue in 1479. He took the cue to create an equestrian portrait to rival Donatello's Gattamelata monument in Padua and the famous ancient statue of Marcus Aurelius in Rome.

Problems involving the bronze casting arose which Verrocchio would not live to solve. After the master sculptor's death in 1488, Alessandro Leopardi, the man who cast the three flagstands in Piazza San Marco, was called back from exile (for fraud) to accomplish the task. This he did expeditiously, also engraving his own signature on the horse's girth and designing the plinth upon which it stands today.

Behind Colleoni's monument rises the **Basilica di Santi Giovanni e Paolo** (open 7:00–12:30 and 15:30–19:30). Its nickname, "San Zanipolo," is derived from the blending of the Venetian names of Sts. John and Paul, to whom it is dedicated.

The church was begun just slightly before the Frari (Walk 2), on a marshy island granted to the Dominican order by Doge Giacomo Tiepolo in 1234; it was not finished until 1430. It is a vast brick structure in Venetian Gothic style, the largest in the city. Because it was built over such a long period of time, the lower section of the façade is not in the same style as the upper. The Greek marble columns flanking the front doors were salvaged from an ancient church on Torcello and incorporated into the design.

The sheer size and scope of this building gave Venetian rulers pause and cause for alarm. In their thinking, no religious structure should ever overpower one of political purpose. No single church—basilica or not—should ever be larger than the chapel of the state. They countered first by connecting the Doges' Palace to St. Mark's Basilica, but this did not live up to their expectations. Finally, it was decided that the Basilica di Santi Giovanni e Paolo would become the burial place of the doges, thus supplanting the structure's religious importance with a political significance. What they created, then, in Giulio Lorenzetti's words, was the "Pantheon of Venetian memories."

When you enter the church, be mindful of the steps just inside the main doors. Immediately, the high nave and apse lit by narrow, double-lancet windows impress you with their celestial beauty. Monuments all around give a clear impression of the development of Venetian sculpture.

Directly on the left is Alessandro Vittoria's *St. Jerome*, a fine example of statuary.

On the south aisle, to the right of the main doors, we find first a monument to Doge Pietro Mocenigo (1485), by Pietro Lombardo, the head of the family that built the façade of the adjoining Scuola Grande di San Marco and the Chiesa di Santa Maria dei Miracoli, which we will visit soon on this walk. The monument is a masterpiece of Renaissance sculpture and a clear representation of life. The conventional, dramatic depiction of death, so common in the Middle Ages, has been abandoned in favor of scenes of human achievement that glorify the existence of the warrior leader.

To our left we find an extraordinary altarpiece by Giovanni Bellini. The polyptych represent Sts. Christopher and Sebastian. Above this is an exquisite Annunciation, one of the finest renditions of the holy scene found anywhere.

Nearby is a memorial to Marcantonio Bragadin, one of Venice's most heroic warriors, who came to a most gruesome end in August 1571 on the island of Crete. Under his leadership Venetians there defended themselves for two years against attacks by Turkish forces. Mustafa led the siege against the Venetians under direct orders from the sultan, who had conquered Constantinople.

While negotiating terms of surrender, Bragadin was attacked by Mustafa, who cut off his ears and nose and imprisoned him for three weeks before his scheduled execution. We can only wish that that was the end of his suffering.

Delirious from his festering wounds, Bragadin was yanked from his cell and dragged around the prison walls with stones on his back. Next, he was hoisted to the yardarm of the Turkish flagship and tortured by the sailors. Finally, he was carried to the place of execution, where he was lashed naked to a column and flayed alive, bearing the ordeal in total silence before expiring as the executioner reached his waist. Once the grim task was complete, he was decapitated, his body drawn and quartered, and his skin stuffed with straw, mounted on the back of a cow, and paraded through the city.

Mustafa carried the skin of Bragadin back to the sultan in Constantinople as a trophy of war. Nine years later, Girolamo Polidoro, one of the few survivors of the siege, stole the skin and returned it to Venice. And on May 18, 1596, it was placed into a leaden casket and set in the niche behind the hero's monumental urn. By merely stopping before the memorial we pay tribute to Bragadin's life. And by retelling his ordeal in these few words we help to keep alive the memory of this martyr.

After walking to the end of the southern aisle, we turn right and confront a true rarity in Venice: a huge, beautiful stained-glass window. Made in 1473 by Murano's master glazier Antonio Lincinio from designs by Bartolomeo Vivarini and Cima da Conegliano, the window has been restored recently, to let all of its color shine through. Like frescoes, large stained-glass artworks are few and far between in Venice. A building's continuous settling and shifting on its pylon foundation usually cracks and crumbles such brittle and delicate surfaces. Luckily, this window has been spared those ravages of time. (It's ironic that in a city so long renowned for its glass, so little of it survives in its churches.)

Directly behind us, beyond the main altar, is the Cappella del Rosario. Alessandro Vittoria was commissioned to design this Chapel of the Rosary, meant to celebrate Venice's victory over the Turks at Lepanto on October 7, 1571 (an interesting coincidence here, since *vittoria* means "victory").

A fire on the night of August 16, 1867, destroyed the original sixteenth-century decoration here. Tragically, works by Tintoretto, Francesco Bassano, Jacopo Palma the Younger—and Giovanni Bellini's *Madonna and Saints* and Titian's *St. Peter*—were lost in the flames.

The present decoration is confined to four great paintings by Paolo Veronese: *The Annunciation, The Adoration of the Shepherds,* and *The Assumption.* Originally from the Chiesa dell'Umiltà, they were transported here and placed in Art Nouveau–style wooden frames by Carlo Lorenzetti in 1932. Unfortunately, a 1958 restoration of these works left too muted Veronese's exceptional color, which was an inspiration to so many eighteenth-century artists.

Fortunately, in this very chapel, a fourth painting by Veronese has been restored more recently—and more successfully. In *The Nativity,* which hangs on the wall opposite the altar, we can experience fully the reds, yellows, and greens as the artist intended them. The figure of the gentleman in the lower right-hand corner is a self-portrait.

Before exiting the chapel, take a moment and gaze upon the face of the Virgin presiding over you. Hers is a peaceful and loving visage.

From the main aisle of the basilica, we see numerous monuments to heroes from Venetian history. And one to a man known more for villainy than heroics.

Buried here in the family vault is Doge Marino Falier, a learned and aristocratic man who was elected to his high office at the age of seventy-seven without ever seeking the honor.

In 1355, after eight months in power, Falier became outraged at a young nobleman who had insulted his wife, and he turned against the entire upper class. With Filippo Calendario (the designer of the Doges' Palace mentioned in Walk 1), Falier conspired to overthrow the Republic and make himself prince, enlisting the help of lower-class workers to accomplish his goal.

Before the movement could even get off the ground, Falier was arrested, forced to confess his crimes, and promptly beheaded for treason. Calendario was strangled for his crimes and strung up between the two red columns on the loggia of the Doges' Palace. Falier suffered further ignominy by being declared persona non grata throughout history. His likeness was removed from the long row of doges' portraits in the Hall of the Great Council in the Doges' Palace, and his name was stricken from all official records.

As we exit the basilica through the main portal, we have, on our right, the Lombardo family's delightful fifteenth-century trompe-l'oeil façade of the **Scuola Grande di San Marco** (Ruskin described this façade as "the most monstrous example of the Grotesque Renaissance which is to be found in Venice; the sculptures on its façade representing masses of diseased figures and swollen fruit."). Once one of Venice's six major *scuole*, San Marco controlled the social and political structures of its district. Today, it is the entrance to Venice's main hospital, the Ospedali Civili. Tintoretto's paintings for the *scuola* can now be seen in the Accademia (Walk 3).

Facing the canal, we exit the *campo* by way of Fondamenta Dandolo to the left; then we cross Ponte Rosso. From this bridge we can look up the entire length of Rio dei Mendicanti and across the broad Canale delle Navi and see the **Cimitero di San Michele.** This island cemetery was created by Napoleon during his reign, and it is here that Venetians are solemnly laid to rest. (For only fifty years' time, however, we are told; their bones are removed to other out-islands to make room for the next generation of deceased.)

Proceed on Calle de le Erbe, cross Ponte de le Erbe, bear right on the *fondamenta*, than left; follow Calle Castelli (a.k.a. Calle Franco la Chiesa) to the **Chiesa di Santa Maria dei Miracoli.**

Air pollution, flooding, and acid rain have taken their

Scuola Grande di San Marco

toll on the exterior stonework of this lovely, human-scale church. Since the mid-1980s, an international association of contributors, the Save Venice Foundation, has been working to repair the damage and arrest the effects of the "marble cancer" that has been steadily dissolving the stone into powder.

According to legend, in 1408, Angelo Auroli, who owned most of the real estate surrounding this *campo*, presented to his neighbors a likeness of the Virgin that was said to have miraculous powers. Shortly thereafter, a collection was begun to raise funds to construct a church in Mary's honor. (This certainly should have helped to raise the property values of Auroli's holdings.)

Pietro Lombardo and his sons, Antonio and Tullio, began construction of the church in 1481 and completed it on December 31, 1489. This jewel of Renaissance Venice, its façade inlaid with polychrome marble and its interior walls lined with panels of gray and rose, combines Tuscan architecture with Byzantine decoration, very much in the way St. Mark's Basilica melds its various elements of structure and ornamentation.

Overhead, the barrel-vaulted ceiling of wood and recessed panels of oil on canvas (in a technique known as *a cassettoni*) presents some fifty portraits of saints, prophets, and patriarchs by the late-sixteenth-century painter Pier Maria Pennacchi. The altar, raised fourteen steps from the main floor, holds the icon of the Madonna said to have worked the miracles (*miracoli*) referred to in the church's name. Today, this church is used only occasionally, usually for weddings of couples from the neighborhood. A fitting place in which to wed, one should think. What marriage nowadays *doesn't* need a "miracle" every now and then?

Back outside, exit behind the church and take Ponte Santa Maria Nova to Campo di Santa Maria Nova. We cross this lovely setting, with its frame shop on the left, diagonally to arrive at Campiello Bruno Crovato già San Canzian. Ahead of us to the right we find the **Chiesa di San Canziano.**

If you enter through the side doors, you will find Tintoretto's stunning *Crucifixion* (1568) in a quiet atmosphere set off by red-and-gold-covered columns and simple crossed arches in the ceiling.

Exit to the right from the front of the building and cross Campo Canzian. Go over Rio dei Santi Apostoli by way of Ponte San Canzian and along Calle de la Malvasia, straight through Campiello de la Cason. Zigzag right then left, and walk toward the back of a church into Campo Drio la Chiesa. Follow the side of the church into Campo

Santi Apostoli. There, amid a surprise of neighborly activity (particularly in late morning), is the entry to the **Chiesa dei Santi Apostoli,** built in the fifteenth century as a chapel for the Corner family.

Its interior is accented by a flat ceiling of fresco and oil. Water trickles over a small fountain on the left. A gold crown floats over the altar. Giovanni Battista Tiepolo's *St. Lucy* hangs on a wall.

This is a close-knit neighborhood, united around the church, and masses here are well attended by the loyal congregation. When certain out-of-towners visit Venice over a weekend, they seek out churches like this in which to attend Sunday services. You may wish to do the same here.

Exit the *campo* to the left of the church front and follow signs indicating "Ca' d'Oro" and "Ferrovia." We will walk about two-thirds the length of **Strada Nova.**

This *rio terà*, originally called "Via Vittorio Emanuele II, was opened in 1871 after extensive demolition brought down houses along the way to fill in the canal and broaden the thoroughfare. It is the primary overland access between the train station and the interior of the city. This sunny and spacious street is busy day and night—with natives not tourists—as the neighborhood is filled with shops where the "real people" of Venice purchase their food and clothing, household appliances and other necessities.

Ahead of us on the left is the picturesque Santa Sofia dock. The *traghetto* that leaves from here is used primarily by natives who cross the Canal Grande each day to shop in the fish and vegetable markets (Walk 2) across the water. The fare is 400 lire; the ferry holds up to sixteen (standing) people, and the ride can be nerve-wracking for anyone lacking confidence in his "sea legs."

Turn left just past the dock onto Calle Ca' d'Oro, and soon you will reach the **Ca' d'Oro** (open 9:00–14:00; Sundays 9:00–13:00; closed Mondays). Its huge wooden door will be locked. You enter the palace through the

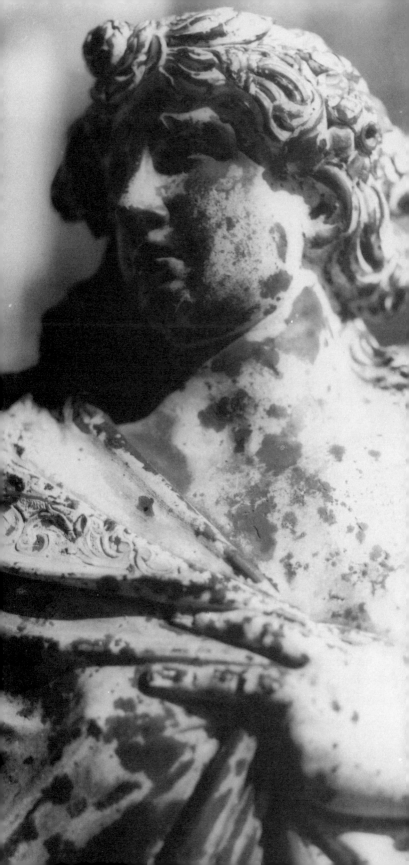

Galleria Giorgio Franchetti, but first walk to the *vaporetto* stop and look at the palace façade and the views up and down the Canal.

During the rise of the Venetian merchant class, before Palladio built showplace villas across the mainland (his Villa Barbaro Maser in Asolo being the finest example), the palaces along the Grand Canal formed the "Gold Coast" of Venice. Their homes combined the latest Gothic style with Byzantine decoration and became the grandest residences in all of Italy. And in its time, the Ca' d'Oro was probably the most beautiful private structure in the world.

Built around 1440 by the brothers Giovanni and Bartolomeo Bon for Marino Contarini, the palace got its name from the extensive gold (*oro*) leaf that once covered the marble tracery on the façade.

During Ruskin's time, the mid-1800s, this palace was severely vandalized by the ballerina Maria Taglioni, who had been given it by the Russian prince Alexander Troubetzkoy, in 1847. She systematically dismantled its interior and sold it off as waste marble.

Baron Giorgio Franchetti, the last private owner, restored the palace in 1896, donated it and his art collection to the state in 1916, and moved to the Ca' Franchetti near the Accademia Bridge (Walk 3). Works by Mantegna, Titian, Vivarini, Bellini, Guardi, Tintoretto, Carpaccio, and Van Dyck are on exhibit inside.

Upon entering, check out the little garden and look through the iron gates at the courtyard, staircase, and elaborate mosaic floor.

Near the top of the stairs, Andrea Mantegna's powerful and terrible *St. Sebastian* startles you with its graphic realism. On this level you will also see remnants of Giorgione's frescoes from the Fondaco dei Tedeschi's façade (Walk 2). The ceiling, with its numerous little angels, *putti*, is fanciful and fun. In a small side room, photographs of a recent restoration show the extensive work done to create this gallery.

If the doors to the small terrace are open, step outside for a moment to meet the many little lions adorning the railing and take in the vista of the Grand Canal.

When you're back on Strada Nova, you will find a number of pizzerias, sandwich shops, and bars that offer very good food at nontourist prices.

Continue walking until you cross Ponte Novo di San Felice. Take an immediate right onto Fondamenta di San Felice and follow it to the end. Turn left by one of only two bridges without railings in all of Venice, Ponte dei Chiodo (the other, Ponte del Diavolo, is on Torcello).

Proceed on Ramo de la Misericordia, cross over Ponte de la Misericordia, and bear right along Fondamenta de la Misericordia. As the signs have led us to believe, we reach the **Misericordia**. This huge brick building—one of the largest in Venice—was once a *scuola grande*. It was built by Jacopo Sansovino, but its façade was never completed. Refurbished in this century, it became the Palasport della Misericordia. The upper floor has been used as a sports arena (it features a basketball court) for many years.

We would be remiss if we did not say more about Sansovino. His name, his architecture, his legacy have enriched every one of our walks. His work has had a profound and everlasting effect on everything Venetian.

He was born Jacopo Tatti in Florence on July 2, 1486. At the age of fifteen, he was apprenticed to the sculptor Andrea Sansovino and trained in the Donatello tradition. Two years later, to honor Andrea, Jacopo took his master's last name.

By 1505, Sansovino was in Rome, having traveled there with his mentor and friend Giuliano da Sangallo. One of Sansovino's first assignments was to restore a series of Vatican statues for Pope Julius II.

Six years later, he was in Florence, carving the statue of St. James the Greater, the first of the twelve apostles he created for the Florentine cathedral's dome. (Michelangelo had been commissioned in 1503 to execute these

statues, but by 1511, he had begun only one, the St. Matthew, and the priests were getting impatient.)

When he returned to Rome in 1518, after completing his assignment in Florence, Sansovino distinguished himself among enlightened circles of Roman society by designing churches and palaces of unsurpassed proportion and detail. The churches of San Marcello and San Giovanni dei Fiorentini are two fine examples.

But his career was rudely cut short in 1527, when Emperor Charles V conquered Rome and sacked the city. Sansovino escaped with very little and arrived in Venice (legend has it) without even enough money to buy a glass of wine.

Luckily, his reputation had preceded him and Sansovino was named the Republic's *Proto*, chief architect— a position of extreme influence and esteem. Immediately, he set to work gracing Venice with his talent and his vision. And he repaid Venice many times over for the honor bestowed on him.

In Walk 1, we saw Sansovino's Libreria Vecchia and learned the story of his imprisonment during its construction, after the ceiling collapsed in 1545. In Walk 2, we visited San Zulian (San Giuliano), a lovely church that experienced a similar problem with its ceiling.

Certain questionable construction techniques aside, Sansovino's work on these buildings gave great pleasure to their sponsors and his ever-increasing number of commissions touched all the districts of the city. From the colossal statues of Neptune and Mars on the Giants' Staircase in the Doges' Palace to the Chiesa di Santa Maria Mater Domini, his work proves strong and Roman-inspired. From the Loggetta of the Campanile, with its beautiful bronze statues of Minerva, Apollo, Mercury, and Peace (Walk 1), to the Palazzo Corner, his attention to detail is unequaled. From the Zecca, the Mint, on the Molo to the breathtaking bronze door of St. Mark's sacristy, Sansovino's sense of harmony and drama is played out for all to appreciate.

Of this master architect and sculptor who had such a profound and lasting effect on Venice, very little else is known. It has been written that Sansovino was something of a dandy, very handsome, with fair hair and a red beard, and that he relished the doting attention he received from women from all walks of life. It has also been suggested that he was hot-tempered and a bit of a braggart. And he must have been a man with an extremely strong constitution, because in later life he survived four debilitating strokes and kept right on working on his commissions. The sixteenth-century biographer Giorgio Vasari wrote that during this time Sansovino limited his diet to fruits and vegetables, often eating "three cucumbers at a time with half a lemon." Apparently, this health-food regimen did some good. The ailing Sansovino lived to be eighty-four years old; he died on September 27, 1570.

Having crossed over the wooden Ponte de l'Abazia, we turn left under the Sottoportego de l'Abazia and proceed along Fondamenta de l'Abazia. Take the first right (opposite the iron-railed bridge at Corte Vecia) and proceed under the arch. From here, we see the cemetery island of San Michele and Murano across the water to the west. Cross the *ponte* and walk along Fondamenta Gasparo Contarini toward the Chiesa della Madonna dell'Orto.

Across the *rio* ahead on the left, notice the stone relief of the man and camel set into the façade of a building. There's a little legend about it: It seems a young Levantine silk merchant came to Venice in the twelfth century to seek his fortune and establish his business. In time, he prospered enough to build this home, **Palazzo Mastelli**, and to send for his wife to join him. "But how shall I find you?" she asked in correspondence through a scribe. "I cannot read." The loving husband promised to adorn their house with the image of a camel so that when she arrived at Piazza San Marco all she had to do was ask directions to the landmark. One hopes she found her way safely and that they lived happily ever after.

During the sixteenth century, this district became one of Europe's leading centers of textile production. Until then, Venetian involvement in the industry remained primarily that of distribution, importation, and exportation. Merchants took their profits from that and had very little to do with the actual manufacture of cloth or clothing. But the discovery of the New World (and the coincidental and simultaneous sacking of Italian mainland cities) changed all that. A chain of seemingly unrelated events brought about Venice's next industrial boom.

Spanish and Portuguese exploration of the Americas broke two monopolies held by Venetian merchants, those of red dye and sugar. The dyestuff was an extract from an Indian wood that the Venetians called *Verzino*, and the control of its distribution was a richly rewarding enterprise. But Portugal discovered an apparently endless supply of this timber—brazilwood—in South America and flooded world markets with an inexpensive alternative to the Venetian commodity.

The same thing happened with sugar. Until the early 1500s, Venetian merchants dominated the market; after all, they owned the island of Cyprus, one of the only places in the known world where sugar cane grew. Then Spanish explorers discovered that the stuff grew like weeds on islands such as Puerto Rico, and once again Venetian profits bottomed out.

To counter these setbacks, Venetians planted cotton (which they called "the plant of gold") on Cyprus and began importing their own dyes into the Lagoon City. Soon a fledgling native textile industry became the strongest single source of Venetian economic and population growth. (Between 1516 and 1565, textile manufacturing expanded tenfold and the population reached an all-time high of more than 200,000.)

Couple these developments with a major influx of mainland refugees escaping foreign invasions of Rome, Florence, and Milan and you can see how Venice continued to flourish through what could have been very lean times. Many of the immigrants were weavers of woolen fabrics who brought with them the tools and skills needed to increase Venice's industrial workforce. As we'll soon learn when we reach the Ghetto, Venice had already become a haven for Jews, who were traditionally the merchants of used clothing. The textile industry became the true sustaining force of Venetian economy. And this area of Venice, because it happened to have the space to ac-

commodate the expansion of factories and populace, became the recipient of many of the rewards.

Soon we reach the **Chiesa della Madonna dell'Orto**
(open 9:30–12:00 and 16:30–19:00). In the fourteenth
century, Fra Tiberio of Parma had this church built to
enshrine a miraculous statue of the Virgin Mary, which
today is found in the adjoining garden, *orto*. Be sure to
look up at the unusual *campanile* with its cupola of Ori-
ental influence. It is one of the most unique bell towers
in Venice.

The church's façade is one of the best-preserved ex-
teriors of Venetian Gothic. Inside the church we see a
wooden-beamed ceiling and carved organ loft, which create an austere yet warm atmosphere. The painting of St.
Christopher and the Child Jesus over the main door is
attributed to Bartolomeo Bon.

Jacopo Robusti, Tintoretto, lived in this neighborhood (his father was a dyer of textiles). His home was
right by the above-mentioned Palazzo Mastelli, at what is
now Campo dei Mori 3399, and the Madonna dell'Orto
was his home parish; he is buried here, according to his
wishes. And his *Presentation of the Virgin*, which was created deliberately to rival Titian's depiction of the same
scene now in the Accademia (Walk 3), hangs close by.
Found here also are his paintings *The Adoration of the
Golden Calf*, *The Last Judgment*, *The Beheading of St. Paul*,
and *The Vision of the Cross to St. Peter*. All of these works
were completed before he began work on San Rocco
(Walk 2).

A stately Madonna by Giovanni Bellini is exhibited
here at the first altar on the left, near the entrance. Use
the coin-operated illumination system to view this painting; it is a real treasure by the master. (To the right of
the entrance, you'll find Cima da Conegliano's *St. John
the Baptist*. It, too, is worthy of note.)

Exit the church and leave the *campo* to the right. Walk
along the *fondamenta*, and near its end go left, over the
little wooden Ponte Loredan, and proceed along Calle Lo-

Madonna and saint

redan. Turn right onto Fondamenta de la Sensa, pass the bridge on the left, cross the one ahead, and the next one, the Ponte de la Malvasia, to the left over the *rio*. You're now on Calle de la Malvasia.

Turn right onto Fondamenta dei Ormesini and cross the black iron bridge (one of the last iron bridges built by the Austrians during their brief rule in the nineteenth century). The two ramshackle structures here were Christian-manned sentry posts that once enforced the midnight-to-sunup curfew that confined all Jews to their quarters every night of their lives. Stepping into Campo del Ghetto Nuovo, we enter the traditional Jewish neighborhood known still today as the **Ghetto.**

It's a pleasant and peaceful square, where neighborhood children play under shady trees and local grown-ups stand in little groups, smiling and nodding at the occasional visitors who happen by. Three hundred years ago, tourists to Venice made special trips to the Ghetto just to see the people who lived here and admire women considered among the most beautiful in the world.

Since about the twelfth century, Jews lived around Venice in secluded little mainland communities, and their business trips into the city were regulated by the issuance of special fourteen-day passes. By 1385, the Republic had wised up enough to allow certain Jews to reside within the city itself, and legend has it that an early Jewish settlement was founded on the island once called Spinalunga. Many believe that it was from this community that the island got its present name, Giudecca (Walk 3), although this is not the case (see page 156). For one hundred years this minority religious group enjoyed slow, steady growth and prosperity under the regulated protection of the Republic.

Actually, Venice was the first Christian government to pass civil laws making it illegal to molest a Jew. No one could seize his property, renege on contracts with him, harm his person, or interfere with his religious practices. This is not to say that Jews were not heavily controlled. The protective laws also regulated most aspects

of their lives, even the types of business they could con-
duct. Still, in many ways, Venice became a haven of security and freedom for Jews from all over the world, and
as they settled here, three main groups developed their
own cultural, economic, and political importance.

The first group, the Levantine Jews, came from the
East and had for centuries lived and traded side by side
with Venetians in Constantinople. They were granted a
kind of Venetian citizenship and, along with Jews from
Crete and Corfu, were licensed to trade on international
markets. (This proved particularly advantageous to Venetian business interests when, in the sixteenth century,
the Ottoman sultan negotiated exclusive financial treaties
between his empire and the Levantine Jews.)

By Venetian edicts, a second group, the "German"
Jews, who came mostly from other Italian cities, were
forbidden to participate in international trade and were
allowed to become only moneylenders (for the relief of
the Venetian poor, and at interest rates always lower than
prime), pawnbrokers, and dealers in used clothing.

The third group, the Western Jews, were sellers of
antique furniture, makers of maps, and printers of their
own religious publications. (Later, these Jews were also
allowed to practice medicine—a profession in which they
excelled—and from that time to the end of the Republic,
the doge's personal physician was almost always Jewish.) The story of their arrival in Venice is especially interesting.

In 1492, the "Most Catholic Majesties" Ferdinand and
Isabella of Spain bowed under papal pressure and ordered all Jews expelled from their domain, threatening to
execute any who remained and did not convert to Christianity. (These converts, known as Marranos, were hated
and mistrusted nonetheless; they were often the targets
of persecution by Spanish Catholics, even as late as the
end of World War II.)

The deadline for this mass exodus was set at August 2, 1492—the same day Christopher Columbus was

scheduled to set sail on his fateful voyage—and the explorer noted in his own log that the harbor around the narrow river Saltés was so crammed with ships carrying Jews that he could not enter the Gulf of Cádiz to begin his westward journey until twenty-four hours later.

This action of Spain's—as well as Portugal's similar expulsion of Jews in 1497—brought a rapid rise in Venice's Jewish population, which the Republic sought to control.

In 1516, Venice cordoned off the site of an old cannon foundry, a *ghetto*—from *gettare*, "to cast (metal)"—and declared that all Venetian Jews were to live in this confined space.

Riccardo Calimani, in *The Ghetto of Venice*, quotes the edict, dated March 29, 1516: "The Jews must all live together in the Corte de Case, which are in the Ghetto near San Girolamo; and in order to prevent their roaming about at night: Let there be built two Gates, on the side of the Old Ghetto where there is a little Bridge, and likewise on the other side of the Bridge, that is one for each of said two places, which Gates shall be opened in the morning at the sound of the Marangona [the Campanile bell], and shall be closed at midnight by four Christian guards appointed and paid by the Jews at the rate deemed suitable by Our Cabinet."

From then on, whenever a Jew left his neighborhood, he was required to wear a special yellow hat (later changed to red). This curfew law remained in effect until Napoleon did away with it in 1797, at which time Jews were free to live wherever they pleased, although most remained where they were.

The houses in the Ghetto were not owned by the Jews, who were forbidden to own real estate (as were all foreigners residing within the Republic). But Jews were granted a special privilege known as the *jus gazaka*. Having various connotations and indicating the presumption of a legal relationship, it granted the right to guaranteed rental conditions valid for a specific person and for a specified amount of time. This right of rented residency, once obtained, could then be inherited, bestowed as a dowry, given away, or sold.

By the end of the seventeenth century and after the completion of the three Ghettos, the Republic of Venice recognized the leadership of the "University," the body that united the three component nationalities as their regular interlocutors.

The leaders, or *parnassim*, were elected by a general assembly, the *Kahal Gadol*, whose number varied from six to twelve. Membership to the council was open to anyone who could afford a tax of twelve ducats. They in turn founded the *Va'ad Katan*—the executive council—whose members served a term of two and a half years.

Each nationality of Jews in Venice had its own assembly. The Germans and Levantines called theirs the *Kahal*; and the Western Jews called theirs the *Talmud Torah*. But it was the University that was ultimately in charge. With considerable independence within the confines of the Ghetto, it regulated taxes, authorized payments, and ran the synagogues and the Jewish cemeteries. Establishing exactly how much tax each person owed on capital and income was difficult, but to avoid resentment, the tax collectors, or *tansadori*, were always selected carefully.

The autonomy of the Ghetto—"a republic within the Republic"—made the appointment of permanent personnel an important function: the *shochet*, or ritual butcher; the *hazan*, or cantor; and the *shammash*, who was in charge of synagogue services.

The rabbis were paid by the community and their contracts ran for a limited term. Supervisors and scribes assisted them in their everyday duties. Being a rabbi in Venice was, of course, a privilege: the Jewish University exerted substantial influence over their own and other Jewish communities throughout Europe.

Within the Ghetto, the synagogues were not the only places where people gathered to pray or study. There were also the *midrashin* and the academies, which were schools founded and supported by groups of individuals or families.

Medicine was an especially popular profession among Jews, thanks to the privileges that the medical class had always enjoyed. From 1517 to 1721, two hundred fifty Jewish medical students graduated from the University of Padua, where they were never segregated. On the contrary, they were assimilated fully into the university environment.

A Jew who went to study at Padua endured a traumatic experience of integration. Thrown from his closed Ghetto into an open student community, he encountered difficulties of language, culture, and religion (especially in the observance of the Sabbath and the preparation and eating of kosher food). To preserve his Jewish identity, the student needed a great capacity for adaptation.

The experience of the Jewish students in Padua, with its benefits and its problems, foreshadowed the more widespread Jewish intellectual revolution in Europe that accompanied the Age of Enlightenment and the later emancipation of the Ghetto. Finally free, Jews were obliged to compete with the world beyond the Ghetto walls.

In the Ghetto of Venice, Hebrew was spoken with many different accents until they eventually absorbed the Venetian language. Little by little, a Judeo-Venetian idiom evolved, of which very few traces remain today and then only in the memory of the oldest Venetian Jews.

Squeezed into so tight an environment, the only place the Jews could go was up. Consequently, the apartment houses in the Ghetto are the tallest in all of Venice. Veritable "skyscrapers" they were, seven, eight, even nine stories high. And with no clear ground on which to build their houses of worship, the Jews constructed their beautiful synagogues on the uppermost floors of their residences. Not only was this a commonsense solution to the problem, it ensured that nothing would stand between their prayers and God in heaven.

During the sixteenth century, the Roman Inquisition

accused the Republic of Venice of not doing its part in burning enough Jewish "heretics" and threatened to punish Venetians severely for their negligence. Venice, uninterested in disturbing its comfortable relationship with its Jewish subjects, calmly responded to the murderous fanatics that Jews were never Christian to begin with and therefore could not ever be "heretics." Venice neatly won the semantic battle and never again heard from the Inquisitors on this matter.

Here in the Campo del Ghetto Nuovo, at no. 2902B, we find the **Museo Giudeo,** the Jewish Museum, which houses the literature, vestments, and religious ornaments of Venetian Jewish culture. If you would like to tour one of the three main synagogues (generally open 10:30–13:00 and 14:30–17:00, with weekday tours beginning at 10:00, 11:00, 15:00, and 16:00), you are well advised to make your reservations here first and check the updated schedules.

In the floors above the Jewish Museum is the **Scola Grande Tedesca,** the German Synagogue. It is the oldest synagogue in Venice, built by the Ashkenazi community in 1528. Outside, two of its five arched windows facing the square have been walled up. Inside, the temple's plan is asymmetrical, a form of twisted ellipse, with the women's gallery set high and close to the ceiling.

To the perpendicular right of the German Synagogue we find the **Sinagogue Canton,** built by the Ashkenazim in 1531. Having undergone numerous restorations over the past four hundred years, this temple was reopened to the public in 1989. The name Canton might be that of the family who sponsored its original construction. Or it might refer to its location on the *campo* (in Venetian, *canton* means "corner"). Then again, it's possible that this synagogue was built by Jews from France (a sixteenth-century map of Venice published in Paris calls the Ghetto the "Canton de Juifs").

Next door, the **Scola Italiana,** built in 1571, is recognizable from the *campo* by its five large windows and the small cupola which is over the pulpit. It may be undergoing restoration at the moment and therefore closed to the public.

Diagonally across the *campo*—lest we forget—are a series of heartwrenching bronze plaques commemorating the Venetian Jews who died at the hands of Mussolini's fascists during World War II.

As we exit the *campo* and cross the *ponte* into Corte Scala, we enter the erroneously named Ghetto Vecchio, the "Old Ghetto," which was not created until 1541. A third, "newest" area, the Ghetto Novissimo, came into being in 1633, when Venice's Jewish population reached its peak of just over 5,000. Today, only about 700 Jews reside in Venice and only about thirty families actually live here in the Ghetto. (To the immediate right is a very good pizzeria, if anyone's hungry.)

Right ahead is the **Sinagogue Spagnola,** the Spanish Synagogue. The largest and most famous, it was enlarged and restored by Baldassare Longhena between 1635 and 1654. It is used for regular services during the summer months. Across the Campiello delle Scole on our left, we find the **Sinagogue Levantina**, the Eastern Synagogue. It was constructed between 1538 and 1561 and is still used for winter services. Each of these temples is lavishly adorned, almost in a classic opera house style, which belies their modest façades and delights the visitor with their grandeur and opulence.

It was in this neighborhood in April 1571 that a most colorful character was born. Leone da Modena was the precocious son of a humble family from Ferrara, and he grew up to become one of Venice's most famous and controversial rabbis.

At the age of two and a half Leone was reading religious tracts, to the amazement of his mother and father. Six months later, he translated passages of the Torah from Hebrew into Italian. A shrewd mathematician with a keen memory, he helped support his family through his skill as a gambler while he was still a boy. And his widening range of interests drove him to open an alchemist's shop some years later; here he devoted many days and nights to trying to turn lead into silver. (According to legend, he paid off any number of gambling debts by convincing his creditors that he'd succeeded!) For these and many other exploits he became reputed throughout Venice, but it was his captivating sermons in the Spanish Synagogue that made him renowned throughout Europe.

In 1616, at the request of the English ambassador to Venice, Leone composed a scholarly treatise on the customs, rites, and laws of Judaism. For the next three hundred years, countless editions of the treatise were printed and reprinted; it was translated from Hebrew into English, French, Dutch, Spanish, German, Italian, and Latin. Possibly more than any other man in history, Leone helped educate the world in the ways of the Jewish religion.

Rabbi Leone died in March 1648, almost seventy-seven years old. In his autobiography he claimed to have practiced twenty-six professions in his lifetime. (So much for Venice's attempts to limit the careers of its Jewish subjects!) He was inventive, intelligent, irreverent, innovative, irascible, infamous, and inspirational. A true son of Venice, Leone da Modena's spirit lives on and on and on.

As we near the end of our walk, we exit Ghetto Vecchio to the right, under Sottoportego del Ghetto (with its old sentry posts), and meet Fondamenta de Cannaregio o de le Guglie.

At no. 975–977, just before the triple-arched bridge designed by Andrea Tirali in 1688, we find the eighteenth-century **Palazzo Surian-Bellotto.** Once the home of the French embassy, it is here, in 1743, that Jean-Jacques Rousseau worked as secretary to the ambassador, Comte de Montaigu. (Rousseau disliked Venice intensely; he complained about everything from its food to its fashions and complimented only its music in his letters home. Of course, his negative reaction to the city may have had something to do with the fact that a love affair here went heartbreakingly wrong, which he later described in great detail in his *Confessions.*)

Keeping the canal on our right, we stroll along the *fondamenta* until we turn left by the bridge onto the scenic Rio Terà San Leonardo. Throughout the day, the fish, fruit, and vegetable markets along here are filled with colorful characters. As we browse down the street, we follow the signs to the Rialto, and pass along Calle del Pistor.

Cross Campiello de l'Anconeta and then the next bridge, onto what now becomes Rio Terà della Maddalena. Cross Ponte San Antonio and Campo Santa Fosca. Walk back down the Strada Nova and return to the Ca' d'Oro *vaporetto* stop. From here, you can return to the Piazza San Marco by taking the no. 1.

It's a lovely, relaxing, twenty-minute ride back to the Piazza down the Canal Grande, one that recalls our first experience upon arriving and entering the city. Only now, our eyes take in the sights with a much richer knowledge of, and appreciation for, everything before us. Over these

four walks, we have seen so much; and yet there is still so, so much left to see, to know, and to share.

Let us promise ourselves here and now to return to this wonderful place and explore these many islands, streets, and canals once again. All too soon we will go back to our "normal lives" at home, but we can do so with the hope that a piece of us will stay behind amid the shimmering Venetian light, to be reclaimed and rejuvenated when we are here in seasons to come.

As we close here, let us quote from the first guide-book of Venice ever published, written by Francesco Sansovino, Jacopo's son, in 1581. He explains the origins of the city's name, Venezia: " '*Veni etiam*': that is to say, 'Come back again and again,' for however many times you come you will always see new and beautiful things."

Finally, we bid farewell to you and this glorious city, using the traditional salutation derived from the Venetian term *schiavo*, which means "I am your slave." It's an altogether fitting acknowledgment to the illustrious city of Venice, don't you think?

Ciao!

Recommended Establishments

Hotels

(MOST EXPENSIVE → LEAST)

Gritti Palace (CIGA hotels): San Marco, Santa Maria del Giglio 2467, tel. 5294611, tlx. 410125 GRITTI

Cipriani: Giudecca 10, tel. 5226480, tlx. 410162 CIPRVE

Monaco & Grand Canal: San Marco, Calle Vallaresso, 1325, tel. 5205044, tlx. 410450 MONACO

Saturnia & International: San Marco, Via XXII Marzo 2398, tel. 5208377, tlx. 410355 SATURN

La Fenice et Des Artistes: San Marco, Campiello de la Fenice 1936, tel. 5232333, tlx. 411150 FENICE

Pausania: Dorsoduro, San Barnaba 2824, tel. 5222083, tlx. 420178 PAUVCE

Flora: San Marco, Calle Bergamaschi 2283A, tel. 5235549, tlx. 410401 FLORA

Accademia: Dorsoduro, Fondamenta Bollani 1058, tel. 5210188

Casa Frollo: Giudecca, Fondamenta Zitelle 50, tel. 5222723

Recommended Establishments

Calcina: Dorsoduro 780, tel. 5206466
Wildner: Castello, Riva degli Schiavoni 4161, tel. 5227463

Restaurants

(MOST EXPENSIVE → LEAST)

Al Graspo de Ua: San Marco 5093, tel. 5200150
Malamocco: Castello 4650, tel. 5227438
Alla Madonna: San Polo 594, tel. 5223824
La Furatola: Dorsoduro 2870A, tel. 5208894
Caffè Orientale: San Polo 2426, tel. 719804
Fiaschetteria Toscana: tel. 5285281
Antiche Carampane: tel. 5240165
Da Remigio: tel. 5230089
Al Baccaretto: tel. 5289336
Sempione: tel. 5226022
Conca d'Oro: tel. 5229293
Bora Bora: tel. 5236583
De Vidi: tel. 5237201

Shops

WOMEN'S CLOTHING
Fendi: San Marco 1474
La Bauta: San Marco 260
La Coupole: San Marco 1678
Vogini: San Marco 1257A
Giorgio Armani: San Marco 1693
Mario Valentino: San Marco 1473
Trussardi: San Marco 695
Enrico Coveri: San Marco 1135A
Gucci: San Marco 258
Cartier: San Marco 606
Hermès: Piazza San Marco 127
Camiceria San Marco: San Marco 1340

MEN'S CLOTHING
Élite: San Marco 284
Duca d'Aosta: San Marco 4946
Gianni Versace: San Marco 1722
Missoni: San Marco 1312B
Ceriello: Campo San Filippo e Giacomo
Corner Shop Sportswear: San Marco 4855
Black Watch: San Marco 4594
Emporio Armani: San Marco 989
Mila Schön: San Marco 4485
Zeta Sport: San Marco 4668
Pettinelli Sport: San Marco 5028
Brocca: 4607 Calle del Teatro o de la Commedia

Chronological Index of Bolded Terms

Walk Four

Bibliography

Arslan, Edoardo. *Venezia Gotica*. Milan: Electa, 1986.

Arthus-Bertrand, Yann, and Patrick Le Guelvout. *Venezia dall'Alto*. Milan: Rizzoli, 1989.

Bergamo, Silvio. *The Frari's Basilica*. Venice: Zanipolo, 1985.

Bertoli, Bruno, and Antonio Niero. *The Mosaics of St. Mark's*. Milan: Electa, 1987.

Boorstin, Daniel J. *The Discoverers: A History of Man's Search to Know His World and Himself*. New York: Vintage, 1983.

Braunstein, Philippe, and Robert Delort. *Venezia: Ritratto Storico di Una Città*, Venice: Stamperia di Venezia, 1981.

Buckton, David, ed. *The Treasury of San Marco, Venice*. Milan: Olivetti, 1984.

Calimani, Riccardo. *The Ghetto of Venice*. Milan: Rusconi, 1988.

Casanova, Giacomo. *Storia della Mia Fuga dai Piombi di Venezia*. Milan: Armando Curcio, 1964.

Costantini, Massimo. *L'Acqua di Venezia*. Venice: Arsenale, 1984.

Bibliography

David, Elizabeth. *Italian Food*. New York: Harper & Row, 1987.

Demus, Otto. *The Mosaics of San Marco*. Chicago and London: University of Chicago Press, 1984.

Evans, Betty. *Venice: Cooking with Betty Evans*. Carmel, CA: Sun Flower Ink, 1978.

Franzoi, Umberto. *Le Prigioni della Repubblica di Venezia*. Venice: Stamperia di Venezia, 1966.

Galliazzo, Vittorio. *I Cavalli di San Marco*. Venice: Canova, 1981.

Guggenheim, Peggy. *Out of This Century: Confessions of an Art Addict*. New York: Universe, 1979.

Hale, J. R., ed. *Renaissance Venice*. London: Faber & Faber, 1973.

Hewison, Robert. *Ruskin and Venice*. London: Thames & Hudson, 1978.

Honour, Hugh. *The Companion Guide to Venice*. New York: Prentice-Hall, 1965, rev. 1983.

Howard, Deborah. *The Architectural History of Venice*. London: B. T. Batsford, 1980.

Hutton, Laurence. *Literary Landmarks of Venice*. New York: Harper & Brothers, 1896.

Janson, H. W. *History of Art*. New York: Prentice-Hall, 1971.

Kent, John. *John Kent's Venice*. London: Viking, 1988.

Lane, Frederick C. *Venice: A Maritime Republic*. Baltimore: Johns Hopkins University Press, 1973.

Lawner, Lynne. *Lives of the Courtesans*. New York: Rizzoli, 1987.

Levy, Monica, and Roberto Peretta. *A Key to Venice*. Milan: Kiwi, 1989.

Lieberman, Ralph. *L'Architettura a Venezia 1450–1540*. Florence: Becocci, 1982.

Links, J. G. *Canaletto and His Patrons*. London: Paul Elek, 1977.

———. *Venice for Pleasure*. New York: Farrar, Straus & Giroux, 1966, rev. 1984.

Lorenzetti, Giulio. *Venice and Its Lagoon*. Trieste: Lint, 1975.

Martineau, Jane, and Charles Hope, eds. *The Genius of Venice 1500–1600*. London: Weidenfeld & Nicolson, 1983.

McCarthy, Mary. *Venice Observed*. New York: Harcourt, Brace & World, 1956, rev. 1963.

Morris, Jan. *The Venetian Empire: A Sea Voyage*. New York: Harcourt Brace Jovanovich, 1980.

Norwich, John Julius, *A History of Venice*. New York: Allen Lane, 1982.

Perocco, Guido. *Tintoretto a S. Rocco*. Venice: Stamperia di Venezia, 1979.

———, and Antonio Salvadori. *Civiltà di Venezia*. Venice: Stamperia di Venezia, 1978.

Pignatti, Terisio, *Venezia: Mille Anni D'Arte*. Venice: Arsenale, 1989.

Puppi, Lionello. *Andrea Palladio*. Milan: Electa, 1973.

———. *Mauro Codussi*. Milan: Electa, 1977.

Ruskin, John. *The Stones of Venice*. New York: Da Capo, 1960.

Salvadori, Antonio. *101 Buildings to See in Venice*. Venice: Canal, 1969.

Unrau, John. *Ruskin and St. Mark's*. London: Thames & Hudson, 1984.

Valcanover, Francesco. *Jacopo Tintoretto e la Scuola Grande di San Rocco*. Venice: Storti, 1983.

Valeri, Diego. *A Sentimental Guide to Venice*. Florence: Sansoni, 1955.

Vidal, Gore. *Vidal in Venice*. New York: Summit, 1985.

Whittick, Arnold, ed. *Ruskin's Venice*. New York: Whitney Library of Design, 1976.

Wolters, Wolfgang. *Storia e Politica nei Dipinti di Palazzo Ducale*. Venice: Arsenale, 1987.

Zanin, Giovanni, ed. *Chiesa S. Giovanni Grisostomo e Santuario Madonna delle Grazie in Venezia*. Venice: Zanin, 1978.

Index

Index

Index

Index

Index

ABOUT THE AUTHORS

Chas Carner, a resident of New York City who considers Italy a second home, is a free-lance writer, lecturer, and producer of documentary films.

Alessandro Giannatasio, a native Venetian, is a professor at the University of Trieste, historical writer, official guide of Venice, and former president of the Association of Tourist Guides.